VIDEO COPYRIGHT

PERMISSIONS

COPYRIGHT INFORMATION BULLETIN SERIES

1. Jerome K. Miller, *Using Copyrighted Videocassettes in Classrooms and Libraries*, 1984 (out of print).

2. Charles W. Vlcek, *Copyright Policy Development: A Resource Book for Educators*, 1987.

3. Jerome K. Miller, *Using Copyrighted Videocassettes in Classrooms, Libraries, and Training Centers*, 1987.

4. Esther R. Sinofsky, *A Copyright Primer for Educational and Industrial Media Producers*, 1988.

5. Jerome K. Miller (Ed.), *Video Copyright Permissions: A Guide to Securing Permission to Retain, Perform, and Transmit Television Programs Videotaped Off the Air.*

VIDEO COPYRIGHT PERMISSIONS:

A GUIDE TO SECURING PERMISSION TO RETAIN, PERFORM, AND TRANSMIT TELEVISION PROGRAMS VIDEOTAPED OFF THE AIR

by

Jerome K. Miller and others

COPYRIGHT INFORMATION SERVICES

Published and distributed by

Copyright Information Services

440 Tucker Ave., PO Box 1460

Friday Harbor, WA 98250-1460

ISBN: 0-914143-13-1

****

Library of Congress Cataloging-in-Publication Data

Video Copyright Permission : a guide to securing permission to retain, perform, and transmit television programs videotaped off the air / Jerome K. Miller, editor.

      p.   cm. -- (Copyright information bulletin ; no. 5)
      Bibliography : p.
      Includes index.
      ISBN 0-914143-13-1

      1. Video recordings--Fair use (Copyright)--United States.

I. Miller, Jerome K. II. Series
KF3030.4.V53   1989
346.7304'82--dc19   88-38960
[347.306482]   CIP

Dedication

To Mary C. Pepin, who helped in a time of need.

Disclaimer

The opinions contained herein
reflect the authors' informed opinions
but do not constitute legal advice.

Introduction

by

Jerome K. Miller

The plan for this book arose as I reviewed my notes and recollections from a speaking trip. Securing permission to retain and use television programs videotaped off the air was a key part of each of my presentations on that trip, as it has been for many years. However, my conversations with experienced educators and librarians revealed that many of them had a weak grasp of the topic or were apprehensive about seeking permission. Part of the problem may stem from an inadequate literature on the topic. One or two items appear to be very useful but the balance of the literature is too obscure or esoteric to be particularly useful to the busy practitioner.[1] This work is intended to fill that void by offering a thorough guide for busy educators and librarians.

Part I sets the stage for the book. It begins with a narrative written by a college media specialist who has been ordered by his administration to maintain a substantial library of programs videotaped off the air. That college has not been caught in its longstanding transgression of the copyright law. Chapter 2 is a brief news account describing a school district that was caught maintaining a library of television programs videotaped off the air.

Some readers may suggest that the first two chapters describe isolated examples and do not reflect current trends in the profession. Although confirming data is not available, years of working with

---

1   A useful work is a 31 page pamphlet: Beda Johnson, *How to
     Acquire Legal Copies of Video Programs: Resource
     Information,* (3d Rev. Ed.; San Diego; Video Resources
     Enterprise, 1987). (4th Rev. Ed., in preparation.)

schools and colleges on various copyright issues leads me to the un-shakable belief that about half of the school districts and colleges in the United States maintain substantial illegal collections of programs videotaped off the air. Although many schools and colleges now ob-serve the copyright law in this matter, the institutions that systemati-cally infringe the copyright law in this matter will not change their practices until the administrators are afraid of being sued. The recent decision in *Anderson v. Brown*[2] suggests that tax-supported institutions may be exempt from prosecution under the doctrine of sovereign im-munity,[3] but the employees can be sued for copyright infringements. Litigation or legislation to abrogate sovereign immunity in regard to copyright infringements by tax-supported agencies may be considered following a recent Copyright Office report on sovereign immunity.[4] Whether or not Congress or the Justice Department move to limit sovereign immunity, there is reason to believe that the successful prosecution of a Radford University employee in *Anderson v. Brown* may encourage the prosecution of additional school and college employees.

Part I closes with two articles summarizing the legal and ethical issues. Chapter 3 provides a synopsis of the ethics statements adopted by key educational associations. Chapter 4 offers an overview of the rights under the copyright law.

Part II provides a nuts-and-bolts review of the process of secur-ing permission to retain and use television programs videotaped off the air. It also identifies several types of programs that may be copied and used without permission.

Part III offers several useful case studies which elaborate on the information in Part II. One article in this section treats the closely-re-lated problem of securing permission to transmit programs through

---

2   *Richard Anderson Photography v. Deborah Brown and Radford University*. US Court of Appeals, 4th Circuit, No. 87-1610. July 20, 1988.
3   Sovereign immunity arises from the eleventh amendment to the US Constitution which exemps state and local govern-ments from many law suits.
4   *Copyright Liability of States and the Eleventh Amendment* (Washington, DC: Government Printing Office, 1988).

closed-circuit television systems. Part IV completes the book with information about establishing an institutional policy, maintaining good records, and securing permission.

It is hoped that as educators and librarians become aware of their responsibility under the copyright law and establish suitable permissions procedures, there might be fewer examples of the illegal activities described in Chapters 1 and 2. That hope may not be realized until more school and college administrators recognize their responsibility under the copyright law and take appropriate steps to assure that the law is observed.

Jerome K. Miller

TABLE OF CONTENTS

Part I :

Background

Chapter 1 :

A Director's Dilemma:

A Case History Of Building A Videotape Library Off The Air

The author asked to remain anonymous for reasons which are obvious from the content of the article. This article was solicited to provide a note of reality about large-scale and persistent copyright infringements. The author writes about his experience in a college, but the events could have taken place in many school districts or universities. The author has worked diligently to bring his college into conformity with the law. His efforts have been undermined by a sequence of administrators who vacillated in the face of demands from the faculty, organized by the television coordinator, to retain this illegal practice. This practice will continue in thousands of schools, colleges, and universities as long as administrators believe they will not be sued for large-scale copyright infringements.

Looking to the past to recall what or how something happened is called history. Whether or not one profits from history may separate those who are successful from others. This history of our college video collection is one of excitement, abuse, and naivety. Copyright questions concerning new media were negotiated in the early 1960's, but it was clearly understood by most that video-taping a program without permission was a questionable practice, while replaying the program year after year was unethical, if not illegal. Nevertheless our college administration and faculty persisted in asking the media center staff to record off the air, store and replay the tapes through the 60s' and 70's, without seeking permission from the copyright holder. Their interpretation of the fair use doctrine was very liberal. Perhaps they were trying to justify a substantive investment in equipment, space, and personnel. The original purpose for developing television facilities was to save money by teaching a large group with fewer faculty. This error of judgment lead to an effort to use the television facility any way possible.

A new media director arrived in the early 70's, and soon after questioned the practice. Whenever articles or conference sessions reminded us of the questionable practice of recording off the air and replaying the programs year after year, we mentioned it to the faculty and the administration. The answer, if any, was an attitude of "We have the right to broadcast signals because the broadcasts were already paid for by the commercials or public money." Another answer had a bit more credence – several of the programs were not available at any price for rental or purchase. In the mid 70's the president of the college issued a lawyer's opinion indicating the illegality of replaying television programs recorded off the air without the permission of the copyright owners. Still, the video library was not erased, nor were the faculty prohibited from requesting replays. Someone must have had doubts about the practice when a list of titles was quietly circulated among the English, History, and Anthropology Departments. The faculty claimed ownership of the tapes and just wanted to share the wealth with colleagues.

The long-awaited copyright revisions act became law in the late 1970's. It clearly spelled out the legal ways one could record television programs off the air and their subsequent use in the classroom. We were still holding hundreds of video tape programs from the 60's and 70's, some on two-inch tape in black-and-white images. We sent another reminder of copyright law to the administration and the faculty, this time with copies of the law and interpretive articles. Once again the order to cease recording and/or replay never came and the practice continued. There was even some attempt to transfer a few titles from the two-inch format to the 3/4 inch format, because the two-inch equipment was obsolete and unrepairable.

Aware of the possible embarrassment, the administration agreed with the media services director to do something positive to avoid possible legal problems. We gained approval to purchase rights to the titles in the video collection and purchase new copies rather than keep programs recorded off the air. Surprisingly the faculty were reluctant even to search the catalogs for programs to substitute for the off-air video programs. After three years of coaxing the faculty to select substitute film and video titles, we located half of the replacement titles needed and those tapes were erased.

Several problems arose when no adequate substitutes could be found for many titles recorded off the air. The answer to this dilemma was not easy. The copyright holders have not always made rights to their works available beyond the television broadcast; therefore, some faculty believe they have a right to retain and replay off-air video tapes of programs they consider valuable to their teaching regardless of the technical violation of the copyright law.

The turning point for purging the questionable video titles came when the obsolete one- and two-inch VCRs finally stopped working and repair parts were not available. Thus, the remaining off-air titles on older formats were unplayable. You would think that would solve the dispute, but the few titles which had been transferred to 3/4 inch tape were still in demand. We were told by the faculty not to discard the old one- and two-inch videotapes, least a replay machine could be found. Again the administration sided with the faculty, and the tapes remained in storage.

This whole scenario should make one wonder about the attitude of college faculty and administration towards the right to materials for teaching. The fair use doctrine explained in the copyright law has clear limits, but somehow our faculty and administrators felt exempt from the law. Is there a hint of civil disobedience in their response to the law? Are the faculty correct to assume the law does not apply to them? What is the responsibility of the copyright holder to make these products available after initial publication or broadcast? What harm is there in keeping productions broadcast over commercial or public airwaves that are not available in film or video format? Why shouldn't the faculty be able to use any broadcast program for their instructional use, at least until the program is made available at reasonable prices and in a reasonable time. Our people believe authors, producers and actors should be flattered to have their programs selected for use in the classroom immediately after broadcast.

This explanation of our situation would not be complete without a comment about the media center staff situation. Politically, the director could not act unilaterally, because of the prolonged practice and the lack of clear directives from superiors. The coordinator of the

3

television services supported off-air recording as long as faculty requested the programs. Of course, as the questionable videotape library grew and faculty became more dependent on the videotapes for their courses, the television coordinator became more important and his position became more secure. As often happens when people become tied to a way of doing things, the solution to the problem doesn't come until the personnel changes or the equipment fails. In this case, the personnel changed and the equipment failed. The underlying question of academic freedom to access whatever is printed or published or broadcast remains unanswered. As more information disappears, becomes lost, or is held off the market after publication or broadcast the more the issue persists. Our college has been deprived of many good programs broadcast before videotape. Since videotape records are available, there has been little effort from the industry to make all of their broadcasts available to educators. At least there is an increased availability today of such sought-after programs as *NOVA, National Geographic Specials, PBS Specials,* etc. Some of these programs can even be ordered prior to broadcast. Will there ever be a time when the broadcasters, advertisers and producers will encourage colleges to videotape off the air and use the program as needed? The example of computer hardware and software producers encouraging student use by giving equipment and programs creates a market for the product? The graduating students become advocates of the system they used in school.

Our historical sketch of off-air recordings for instructional purposes is presented to inform the reader, raise questions about information access for instruction, and provide a stimulus for discussion about new technology. New technology can store and retrieve vast amounts of information in a very short period. Another question for the future is the availability of print and photographic collections and archives for use by the producers of video disk, CD-ROM or other electronic systems. What will the faculty want to store and retrieve from visual collections? Will they have the right to reproduce visuals on their equipment for replay in the classroom? Changing formats and selecting materials for instruction are almost becoming one in the same operation in the electronic classroom.

Chapter 2 :

El Dorado Union School District Complies With The Law[1]

"Thank you very much for bringing to our attention the lack of full compliance with copyright laws existing in our district ... I have looked into the matter and the following is my response...," wrote David J. Murphy, Superintendent of El Dorado Union School District in a May 2, 1988 letter to Allen Dohra (Barr Films), Chairman of AIME's Copyright Committee.

In October, 1987, Dohra reported to the AIME membership that he was working on a possible violation of the copyright law in a California school district. Programs were apparently taped off air illegally and promoted to other buildings in the district in a catalog.

Dohra is pleased to share the positive results of AIME's efforts in this case. It shows the effectiveness of AIME in the fight against copyright violation.

Superintendent Murphy's letter continued with his plan of action:

1. The Superintendent has met with all librarians and

---

1   Reprinted by permission from *AIME News*, Aug., 1988, p 1-2.

principals to ensure that district policy and lawful procedures regarding the copying of programs from T.V. are being followed, to institute corrective procedures to review all video material, and to eliminate any which were not clearly reproduced and retained according to lawful procedures.

2. The Superintendent has personally conferred with each librarian about their violation and sent letters of reprimand to those employees who were not in compliance with district policies, procedures, and the law related to this area.

3 Only those video tapes which clearly have been reproduced in a legal way and used in a legal way are to be retained by school libraries...

4. All catalogs which listed any materials not legally reproduced have been removed from circulation and destroyed.

5. Librarians have sent memos to all staff to help them understand the law regarding the use of videotapes...

6. The Superintendent has personally visited and inspected each library in the district to be sure that we are only in possession of those tapes which conform to copyright laws.

7. As Chairman of the ACSA State Committee of Secondary School Principals, the Superintendent placed on the committee's agenda the issue of the copyright laws and violations by schools. At that committee meeting, the Superintendent, as the Chairman, discussed the information related to the legal and illegal copying of programs from T.V. He emphasized to each committee member the importance of following the law and the legitimacy of the concerns by private enterprise. He gave committee members instructions to distribute this information to their librarians and other region principals...

8. The Superintendent has purchased a video tape from AIME to assist the District's efforts to keep staff informed about the existing copyright laws, their importance, and the legitimacy of the private sector's concerns.

9. Annually, an inservice for key district people, including reprographics personnel and librarians, will be conducted to ensure everyone's understanding and compliance with the copyright laws. Violations will be subject to sanctions by the District...

Thanks to your helpful assistance and your phone call to me, I do not feel we will have any further difficulty in this area. ...Sincerely, David J. Murphy, District Superintendent.

For more information, contact Allen Dohra (Barr Films), 818/338- 7878 or Bev Brink 319/245-1361.

Chapter 3 :

Professional Ethics And The "I Won't Get Caught" Attitude

by

John A. Davis

"If you don't look for trouble,

it probably won't look for you!"

    "Ethics" is a concept that is seldom invoked in copyright discussions, yet its relevance is readily demonstrable. Webster's defines "ethics" as "the discipline dealing with what is good and bad and with moral duty and obligation" and the "principles of conduct governing an individual or a group.[1]" When the "moral duty" of a group can significantly impact the well-being and quality of life of a great many people, the principles to which that group subscribes should be a matter of general concern. Thus "ethics" are clearly appropriate for members of the medical, counseling, legal, and education professions.

---

1   Webster's Seventh New Collegiate Dictionary. Springfield, MA: G. & C. Merriam Company. p. 285.

The National Education Association (NEA) and the Association for Educational Communications & Technology (AECT) verify that educators are among those groups that recognize moral duty and obligation. These professional associations publish "Codes of Ethics" to which their members are committed as a condition of membership in the Association.

Having established this, let's examine three hypothetical cases involving videotapes and copyright.

Case A

A conscientious teacher, regarded as exemplary in her ability to create an atmosphere of excitement and discovery in her classroom, prepares her students for a vicarious journey to another time and place where they will experience life in a culture quite different from their own. Using research-proven media teaching techniques, the teacher builds her students' curiosity and enthusiasm for what they are about to experience, helps them develop terms and questions to watch for, and then directs their attention to the television screen to watch a television program she videotaped during its broadcast. The first thing the students see on the screen is an announcement stating "For home use only. Federal copyright law prohibits the unauthorized exhibition of this videotape."

Case B

A community college instructor intent on stimulating his students' interest in science, displays a videocassette report taken from a commercial broadcasting network public affairs program. No network identification appears on the tape, but the voice of the famous narrator is recognizable. The instructor mentions that he got the tape two years ago from a colleague at another campus (much as they freely exchange computer disks).

Case C

A professor calls her university media center to request assistance in obtaining a videorecording of a program that is scheduled for broadcast within a few days. The media center makes arrangements to

10

videorecord the program and initiate the process of acquiring a license to retain the tape.

Analysis

Now, what are some probable facts about these three cases? Technically a "home use only" videotape MAY be used in the classroom under Section 110(1) of the Copyright Law. Programs recorded off-air in the home are "legal" copies — for home use, but when brought to the classroom, their status changes. They may be evaluated for forty-five days for possible acquisition by the educational institution, at the end of which time the license must have been ordered or the tape removed/erased. This is the procedure in use by the college professor in Case C, and one the teacher in Case A SHOULD use.

The recording taken from a network public affairs program (Case B) can be subject to the same kind of licensing arrangement. Except for "Pay TV" broadcasts, virtually everything broadcast on television can be obtained for classroom use through the procedures described in the "Guidelines for off-air Recording of Broadcast Programming for Educational Purposes." It makes no difference that the tape in this case came from a colleague at another campus; the guidelines apply whenever an off-air videorecording is used in the classroom.

Very few programs broadcast by the Public Broadcasting System are in the "public domain," even though local station personnel may assure to the contrary. Many PBS programs are tied up in contracts with major producers/distributors (such as Time-Life), and are as tightly guarded as most commercial network programs.

It would, of course, be a rare classroom where all this was explained to students prior to their viewing a videotape. But one possible consequence could be that in addition to the vicarious educational experience planned by the teacher, the students "learn" that (A) the copyright law does not apply to the classroom, or (B) it's okay to ignore the copyright law because the FBI is unlikely to visit this classroom to catch such offenses. Neither conclusion is accurate.

Moreover, sidestepping the copyright law puts at a disadvantage those faculty members who conscientiously try to follow the law. Colleagues may communicate to their students the attitude that the law-abider is unrealistic in imposing bureaucratic roadblocks on the use of information that "should" be freely available.

Educators' Ethics

The preamble to NEA's Code of Ethics of the Education Profession, to which teachers subscribe when they become members of their local Education Associations, states that "The educator accepts the responsibility to adhere to the highest ethical standards.[2]" If it IS within these ethical standards to appropriate information resources without paying for them, would it not be similarly ethical to rustle a farmer's livestock in order to let students see a cow first hand?

How can a "model" teacher casually overlook a cautionary announcement at the head of the videotape, and know little or nothing about the forty-five day evaluation rule? Is it because the education profession so values wide and creative use of information resources that educators believe that information resources are not really "owned" by anyone? Is the term "intellectual property rights" an oxymoron?

The Association for Educational Communications and Technology (AECT) is a professional association which includes among its members both users and producers of videotapes and other educational media. AECT was originally the Department of Audio-visual Instruction (DAVI) of the National Education Association, whose members accepted the Code of Ethics of the Education Profession. When the NEA became primarily an organization for classroom teachers, the opportunity existed for DAVI to address special concerns of educational media professionals. The AECT Code of Ethics was developed in the context of aggressive efforts by an ad hoc committee of educators to influence the writing of the 1976 Copyright Law to recognize the needs of both information "creators" and users of that information. The code adopted by AECT in 1974 admonishes members to "inform users of the stipulations and interpretations of the

---

2   National Education Association. "Code of Ethics of the Education Profession." Adopted by 1975 Representative Assembly.

copyright law and other laws affecting the profession and encourage compliance." Members are also enjoined to "follow sound professional procedures for evaluation and selection of materials and equipment" and "promote current and sound professional practices in the use of technology in education."[3]

The Consortium of University Film Centers (CUFC) is an organization of university-related agencies that circulate film and videotape resources to the public, on a short-term rental basis. CUFC subscribes to and supports the efforts of the Television Licensing Center. Annual circulation data from Consortium institutions has shown DECREASES in the rental of films and videotapes each year for the past several years. There are several possible explanations — (A) schools are using fewer films and videotapes [unlikely], (B) schools are buying their own tapes [may be true], (C) schools have to buy fewer resources because teachers are building libraries of programs videotaped off the air [the worst fear of producer/distributors].

There are anecdotal reports of educators bringing tapes they record off-air to the school and depositing them in the media center for general use. Such behavior is laudable when it is altruistic sharing of the educator's personal resources. However, it is not laudable when the altruism is the videotape producer's—without that producer's knowledge!

A solution to the problem is simple, and effective if universally applied. Each educational district or institution should have a copyright policy to guide educators in these complicated matters. Districts and institutions also should provide a simple, straight-forward way for educators to request assistance in recording desired programs off the air, and instituting evaluation and licensing procedures in accordance with Section 110.[4] Then the use of these videotape resources is both legal, ethical, and honest.

---

3   Association for Educational Communications & Technology, "AECT Code of Etchics," 1974.

4   For preparing copyright policies, see Charles W. Vlcek, *Copyright Policy Development: A Resource Guide for Educators,* Friday Harbor, WA: Copyright Information Services, 1987.

Chapter 4 :

Basic Legal Rights

by

Jerome K. Miller

The first federal copyright law passed in 1790 and has been revised many times. The primary purpose of the copyright law is to protect authors' rights. The Copyright Revision Act of 1976 expanded authors' rights by giving film and video producers substantial control over the reproduction and use of their creative works:

Sect. 106. Exclusive rights in copyrighted works

Subject to sections 107 through 118, the owner of copyright under this title has the exclusive rights to do and to authorize any of the following:

(1) to reproduce the copyrighted work in copies or phonorecords;

(2) to prepare derivative works based upon the copyrighted work;

(3) to distribute copies or phonorecords of the copyrighted work to the public by sale or other transfer of ownership, or by rental, lease, or lending;

(4) in the case of literary, musical, dramatic, and choreographic works, pantomimes, and motion pictures and other audiovisual works, to perform the copyrighted work publicly; and

(5) in the case of literary, musical, dramatic, and choreographic works, pantomimes, and pictorial, graphic, or sculptural works, including the individual images of a motion picture or other audiovisual work, to display the copyrighted work publicly. [1]

The first right restricts reproductions of copyrighted works. The second right gives proprietors control over derivative works, such as new editions of books, films based on books, and clothing and posters displaying cartoon characters. The third right, the "right of first publication," enables proprietors to keep products off the market. This right expires when the work legitimately enters the market — through sale, lease, or lending.

The fourth right was substantially rewritten in the 1976 act. It now permits copyright owners to control most performances (showings) of their copyrighted works. (This issue is addressed in the next paragraph.) The fifth right provides a similar control on displays of copyrighted art works.

PERFORMANCE RIGHTS

When the copyright act was revised in 1976, the for-profit- performance-in-public limitation in the 1909 act was replaced with subsections four and five, described above. Although the new copyright act enhanced the proprietors' right to control performances and displays, it also authorized certain exemptions. The key exemption for educators appears in Sect. 110(1). That exemption authorizes almost all types of performances and displays in face-to-face teaching in nonprofit educational institutions.

Sect. 110. Limitations on exclusive rights: Exemption of certain performances and displays

---

1   Title 17, *U.S. Code*, Sect. 106 (Hereafter cited as Copyright Act.)

Notwithstanding the provisions of section 106, the following are not infringements of copyright:

(1) performance or display of a work by instructors or pupils in the course of face-to-face teaching activities of a nonprofit educational institution, in a classroom or similar place devoted to instruction, unless, in the case of a motion picture or other audiovisual work, the performance, or the display of individual images, is given by means of a copy that was not lawfully made under this title, and that the person responsible for the performance knew or had reason to believe was not lawfully made; .... [2]

The House of Representatives committee report that accompanied the copyright act defines several key phrases:

The "teaching activities" exempted by the clause encompass systematic instruction of a very wide variety of subjects, but they do not include performances or displays, whatever their cultural value or intellectual appeal, that are given for recreation or entertainment of any part of their audience. [3]

"[I]n the course of face-to-face teaching activities" is intended to exclude broadcasting or other transmissions from an outside location into classrooms, whether radio or television and whether open or closed circuit. However, as long as the instructor and pupils are in the same building or general area, the exemption would extend to the use of devices for amplifying or reproducing sounds and for projecting visual images. [4]

Instructors or pupils. — the performance or display must be "by instructors or pupils," thus ruling out performances by actors, singers, or instrumentalists brought in from outside the school to put on a program. However, the term "instructors" would be broad enough to include

2   Copyright Act, Sect. 110.
3   House Report, Sect. 110.1
4   Ibid.

guest lecturers if their instructional activities remain confined to classroom situations. In general, the term "pupils" refers to the enrolled members of a class. [5]

Classroom or similar place. — the teaching activities exempted by the clause must take place "in a classroom or similar place devoted to instruction." For example, performances in an auditorium or stadium during a school assembly, graduation ceremony, class play, or sporting event, where the audience is not confined to the members of a particular class, would fall outside the scope of clause (4) of section 110. The "similar place," referred to in clause (1), is a place "devoted to instruction" in the same way a classroom is; common examples would include a studio, a workshop, a gymnasium, a training field, a library, the stage of an auditorium, or the auditorium itself, if it is actually used as a classroom for systematic instructional activities. [6]

Further clarification appears in The Supplementary Report of the Register of Copyrights on the General Revision of the U.S. Copyright Law: 1965 Bill:

[T]hat the word "institution," while broad enough to cover a wide range of establishments engaging in teaching activities, is not intended to cover "organizations," "foundations," "associations," or similar "educational" groups not primarily and directly engaged in instruction. [7]

To summarize, Sect. 110(1) authorizes the performance and display of any copyrighted work in face-to-face teaching, but it imposes some limitations:

---

5   Ibid.
6   Ibid.
7   U.S. House of Representatives. *Copyright Law Revision*, Part 6 - *Supplementary Report of the Register of Copyrights on the General Revision of the U.S. Copyright Law:* 1965 (Washington, D.C.: Government Printing Office, 1965), p. 37. (Hereafter: Register's Report.)

1. Performances and displays of audiovisual works must be made from legitimate copies;

2. Performances and displays must be part of a systematic course of instruction and not for the entertainment, recreation or cultural value of any part of the audience;

3. Performances and displays must be given by the instructors or pupils or by guest lecturers;

4. Performances and displays must be given in classrooms or other places devoted to instruction;

5. Performances and displays must be part of the teaching activities of nonprofit educational institutions; and

6. Attendance is limited to the instructors and pupils.

These six provisions are simple enough to be readily applied to nonprofit schools, colleges, and universities. But the law is not always as simple as it appears, especially in the application of the sixth criterion, "nonprofit educational institution," which is not defined in the law. This raises interesting questions about other nonprofit agencies which are better addressed elsewhere. [8]

EDUCATIONAL TRANSMISSIONS

Educators continue to raise questions about the legality of transmitting videocassettes to classes through closed-circuit transmission systems. The copyright proprietors insist that privilege is reserved to them in Sect. 110(2), but educators cite the same section of the law, plus other sources, to authorize closed-circuit instructional transmissions. The issue is confusing, but it can be resolved through a close reading of the law:

Sect. 110. Limitations on exclusive rights: Exemption of certain performances and displays

8   See Miller, *Using Copyrighted Videocassettes* 2d ed, Chapter 5.

Notwithstanding the provisions of section 106, the following are not infringements of copyright:

. . . .

(2) performance of a nondramatic literary or musical work or display of a work, by or in the course of a transmission, if —

(A) the performance or display is a regular part of the systematic instructional activities of a governmental body or a nonprofit educational institution; and

(B) the performance or display is directly related and of material assistance to the teaching content of the transmission; .... [9]

At first glance, this appears to authorize instructional transmissions through open- and closed-circuit systems. The confusion arises from the definition of the key phrases: nondramatic works, literary works, and musical works. Dramatic, nondramatic and musical, are not defined in the law, but they are clear enough without further definition. The restriction on performing videocassettes appears in the innocuous phrase, "literary work," which is defined in the law:

"Literary works" are works, other than audiovisual works, expressed in words, numbers, or other verbal or numerical symbols or indicia, regardless of the nature of the material objects, such as books, periodicals, manuscripts, phonorecords, films, tapes, disks, or cards, in which they are embodied. [10]

The limitation is in the first eight words: "literary works are works, other than audiovisual works...." Because of this clause, educational transmissions are limited to nondramatic literary or musical works — and audiovisual works are excluded by definition from this category.

---

9   Copyright Act, Sect. 110(2).
10   Ibid., Sect. 101.

Educators also cite the second sentence of the following quotation from the House report to authorize in-building and campus-wide instructional transmissions:

> "[I]n the course of face-to-face teaching activities" is intended to exclude broadcasting or other transmissions from an outside location into classrooms, whether radio or television and whether open or closed circuit. However, as long as the instructor and pupils are in the same building or general area, the exemption would extend to the use of devices for amplifying or reproducing sounds and for projecting visual images. [11]

Some interpret the second sentence as a modification of the restriction on video transmissions in Sect. 110(2). No one seems to know what the committee intended when it wrote that sentence. Whatever its purpose, this interesting piece of legislative history does not supersede the law, therefore, copyrighted programs cannot be transmitted through closed-circuit transmission systems without a license. Although these transmission rights are reserved, many educational film and video distributors grant closed-circuit, educational transmission licenses free upon request. Other firms charge a small fee for transmission licenses.

SHOWINGS AT BENEFIT PERFORMANCES

Educators sometimes suggest that the benefit performance exemption in Sect. 110(4) authorizes some video performances. A quick glance at the law suggests that interpretation, but as in the preceding paragraph, the definition of "literary work," blocks that interpretation. The act states:

> Sect. 110. Limitations on exclusive rights: Exemptions of certain performances and displays
>
> Notwithstanding the provisions of section 106, the following are not infringements of copyright:
>
> . . . .

---

11   House Report, Sect. 110.

(4) performance of a nondramatic literary or musical work otherwise than in a transmission to the public, without any purpose of direct or indirect commercial advantage and without payment of any fee or other compensation for the performance to any of its performances, promoters, or organizers, if —

(A) there is no direct or indirect admission charge; or

(B) the proceeds, after deducting the reasonable costs of producing the performance, are used exclusively for educational, religious, or charitable purposes and not for private financial gain.... [12]

This is the legal basis for most free performances, such as library storytelling and student concerts. However, as in the preceding paragraph, the definition of "literary work," prevents any type of video performance, regardless of its instructional or cultural value.

SHOWINGS IN RESIDENCE-HALL LOUNGES

The 1987 annual conference of the Association of College and University Residence Hall Officers International included two programs on copyright restrictions on video performances in residence hall lounges. It was reported there that several universities have received cease-and-desist letters as a result of residence hall video performances. Some universities, such as the University of Southern California, immediately terminated all video performances in residence hall lounges. Many universities now acquire nontheatrical public performance licenses authorizing performances in residence hall lounges.

The question arises about residence halls being the students' home and the application of the home-use exemption to residence halls. Students who have videodisc or videocassette recorders in their private rooms are clearly entitled to use the machines under the home-use exemption. On the other hand, there is little question that performances in residence halls that are accessible to non-residents or a large

---

12   Copyright Act, Sect. 110(4).

number of residents are public performances and require a license. Two firms, Films Inc. and Swank Audio-Visuals, sell a variety of licenses in this market and there seems to be no justification for continuing unlicensed video performances.

The difficult question centers on video performances in small lounges accessible to a limited number of students. Many of these lounges are only accessible to the students living in adjacent rooms. Residence hall administrators argue that recent court cases affecting residence hall privacy make these small lounges part of the students' private quarters. The law seems unclear on this point. Some administrators buy licenses for video performances in large lounges but permit unlicensed video performances in small lounges, where access is limited to a few residents who have a key to that lounge.

THE RIGHT TO RECORD OFF THE AIR

The copyright law does not authorize videotaping programs off the air. The off air exemption is contained in the "Guidelines for Off-air Recording of Broadcast Programming for Educational Purposes." (The document is reproduced in Appendix A.) The document was developed at the encouragement of Rep. Robert W. Kastenmeier, the chairman of the House of Representatives Subcommittee on the Courts, Civil Liberties and the Administration of Justice. (That subcommittee supervises copyright bills in the House of Representatives.) The guidelines were expected to accompany the other fair-use guidelines which appeared in the congressional reports accompanying the Copyright Revision Act of 1976, but the interested parties could not arrive at an agreement in time for the document to be included in the congressional reports. After two years of negotiation, the representatives of education, labor, and industry reached a compromise and the document was published in the *Congressional Record* as the House subcommittee's "understanding" of what the courts would regard as a fair use. [13] Although none of the fair-use guidelines have the force of law, it is generally believed that they will be considered by the courts in determining copyright infringement cases involving videotaping off the air for educational purposes.

---

13 "Guidelines for Off-Air Recording of Broadcast Programming for Educational Purposes," *Congressional Record*, Oct. 14, 1981, p. E4751.

The guidelines are fairly simple to apply and may be divided into nine points:

1. The guidelines apply only to broadcast programs, including broadcast programs transmitted simultaneously by cable. They do not apply to non-broadcast programs available from cable television services, including ESPN, C-Span, Home Box Office, etc.

2. All copies must be made at the request of a teacher and not at the instigation of an administrator, librarian, or media specialist.

3. A teacher may not have a program copied more than once, no matter how frequently it is rebroadcast.

4. The copies may be used in the classroom for the first ten "teaching days" after the broadcast. "Teaching days" are days in which classes meet, excluding holidays, examination days, and days when the school is closed due to storms, strikes, etc.

5. The copies may be retained for forty-five days for evaluation.

6. The programs may be duplicated for use by other teachers, so long as the other criteria are met.

7. A teacher may show a program to several classes, if that is appropriate, and a program may be shown to a class twice, the second time for reinforcement.

8. All copies must include the copyright notice that appeared in the program.

9. A teacher may show all or part of a program to a class, but the program may not be edited and two or more programs may not be combined.

The copyright law and the related documents were developed as a compromise between the users and owners of copyrighted programs. Educators and librarians should use the rights that were granted to them, but when they have exhausted their rights, they should honor the rights of the copyright owners. This means seeking permission, and being prepared to pay for additional rights.

Appendix A

FAIR USE GUIDELINES FOR

VIDEOTAPING OFF THE AIR

In March of 1979, Congressman Robert Kastenmeier, chairman of the House Subcommittee on Courts, Civil Liberties, and Administration of Justice, appointed a Negotiating Committee consisting of representatives of education organizations, copyright proprietors, and creative guild and unions. The following guidelines reflect the Negotiating Committee's consensus as to the application of "fair use" to the recording, retention, and use of television broadcast programs for educational purposes. They specify periods of retention and use of such off-air recordings in classrooms and similar places devoted to instruction and for homebound instruction. The purpose of establishing these guidelines is to provide standards for both owners and users of copyrighted television programs.

GUIDELINES FOR OFF-AIR RECORDING OF BROADCAST PROGRAMMING FOR EDUCATIONAL PURPOSES

1. The guidelines were developed to apply only to off-air recording by nonprofit educational institutions.

2. A broadcast program may be recorded off-air simultaneously with broadcast transmission (including simultaneous cable retransmission) and retained by a nonprofit educational institution for a period not to exceed the first forty-five (45) consecutive calendar days after date of recording. Upon conclusion of such retention period, all off-air recordings must be erased or destroyed immediately. "Broadcast programs" are television programs transmitted by television stations for reception by the general public without charge.

3. Off-air recordings may be used once by individual teachers in the course of relevant teaching activities, and repeated once only when instructional reinforcement is necessary, in classrooms and similar places devoted to instruction within a single building, cluster or campus, as well as in the homes of students receiving formalized home instruction, during the first ten (10) consecutive school days in the forty-five (45) day calendar day retention period. "School days" are school session days — not counting weekends, holidays, vacations, examination periods, and other scheduled interruptions — within the forty-five (45) calendar day retention period.

4. Off-air recordings may be made only at the request of and used by individual teachers, and may not be regularly recorded in anticipation of requests. No broadcast program may be recorded off-air more than once at the request of the same teacher, regardless of the number of times the program may be broadcast.

5. A limited number of copies may be reproduced from each off- air recording to meet the legitimate needs of teachers under these guidelines. Each such additional copy shall be subject to all provision governing the original recording.

6. After the first ten (10) consecutive school days, off-air recordings may be used up to the end of the forty-five (45) calendar day retention period only for teacher evaluation purposes i.e., to determine whether or not to include the broadcast program in the teaching curriculum, and may not be used in the recording institution for student exhibition or any other non-evaluation purpose without authorization.

7. Off-air recordings need not be used in their entirety, but the recorded programs may not be altered from their original content. Off-air recordings may not be physically or electronically combined or merged to constitute teaching anthologies or compilations.

8. All copies of off-air recording must include the copyright notice on the broadcast program as recorded.

9. Educational institutions are expected to establish appropriate control procedures to maintain the integrity of these guidelines.

Part II :

The Nuts and Bolts of Securing Permission

Chapter 5 :

Living With The Copyright Law

by

M. Patricia Webb

The copyright law and its various interpretations and applications can be interpreted as strictly or as leniently as anyone chooses. That is, they can be practically ignored by an organization that feels it is too small to be a threat to anyone OR they can be so strictly interpreted that they strangle an instructional staff's creativity and innovative thinking. Somewhere between those extremes each of us must find the place most comfortable for our particular needs and sphere of influence. Ideally, the goal for each of us is to operate under the premise that our tasks are to keep the faculty and staff aware of their rights and limitations as well as to protect the institution.

Tarrant County Junior College has made a concentrated effort to develop a workable system of respect for both the copyright law and the needs of the professional instructional staff. As Coordinator of Instructional Media for the Northeast Campus, I would like to share with you the procedures in effect when I joined the staff in November, 1987. It was firmly in place when I arrived, and it works quite well.

Different needs arise from different disciplines. The basic copyright law provides both broad and yet specific guidelines. Instructors may see ways to meet their needs in a different manner. Lacking an organized approach, interpretation becomes much like the story of the blind men describing the elephant.

The Northeast Campus of Tarrant County Junior College serves over 9,000 students with a full-time faculty of 148 and a part-time instructional faculty of 184. The diverse nature of the instructional programs on each campus reflects the needs of the surrounding communities. Thus, programs offered on Northeast may differ from those offered on the other two TCJC campuses.

With this in mind, each campus is encouraged to develop its own approach to meeting faculty needs by providing specific support services indigenous to each respective campus. In addition, each media center is dedicated to providing leadership in instructional technology.

Copyright Awareness

Sensitivity to the need for an awareness of copyright laws and how they apply to the instructional situation began in the mid seventies. Previously, permission for backup copies of slides and filmstrip programs were made automatically to protect the masters "until replacements could be ordered" without realizing that the copyright laws might be in jeopardy. As awareness of the law was heightened and instructional utilization increased, it became apparent that a systematic approach was needed.

Copyright Policy Statement

Every organization that uses copyrighted materials for instructional purposes needs a written copyright policy. Such a policy recognizes that the copyright law exists and that the organization tries to observe it. The district copyright policy appears in the district policies and procedures manual, which is available to every member of the TCJC family.

Copyright Resource Person

At Tarrant County Junior College-Northeast, Robinel McDaniel, the Media Center's Supervisor of Reference and Scheduling serves as the copyright resource person. She knows the faculty and takes an almost proprietary attitude about protecting them from themselves. Further, she is protective of the available materials and how they will be used and has trained her staff to be equally observant. Her approach to the issues involving copyright is paternalistic.

The operant philosophy is an adult to adult treatment — that is, we refuse to be a policing agency. Thus, we advise, recommend, and assist in our ongoing efforts to help instructors meet their respective needs within the current accepted interpretations of the existing law. However, the resource person does not make interpretations of the law. Instead she locates the opinions of experts in the field that fit given circumstances, particularly when a situation arises that is not specifically addressed in the law.

Sometimes this involves alerting the faculty to specific limitations, offering them options that they might not have considered. At all times this copyright resource person works with the full support of the Dean of Learning Resources while representing him; the Media Center; and the institution

Resource Materials

A variety of print and nonprint materials are available to the designated copyright resource person. She utilizes them as reference as well as to assist faculty in recognizing their rights to various materials. These materials involve video and audio cassettes as well as printed materials. These materials also provide the basis for faculty in-service programs as well as for independent research.

Duties

Specific activities involving copyright are difficult to identify as such since they are considered part of the duties of the reference personnel. Efforts to meet the needs of instructors usually can be grouped into three general areas of correspondence.

1. Writing for permission to make backup copies of audio cassettes in slide and filmstrip programs until a replacement copy can be purchased.

2. Writing for permission to change formats, e.g. U-matic to Beta videotape or audio record disks to cassette tapes.

3. Writing for permission to adapt materials into collections that meet an instructor's specific objectives, e.g. illustrations in books incorporated in an instructor's instructional slide program

Seeking Additional Permission

Requesting copyright release at the time of purchase does not work as well as making requests for specific permissions. Approval is more likely to come as a follow-up request after purchase when a specific need not covered in the original purchase agreement arises.

Telephone calls are a fast method that is often successful. However, it is desirable to send two copies of a follow-up letter summarizing any oral agreement. The letter should stipulate the agreed upon permissions and any restrictions or limitations. One copy of the letter should be signed and returned by the copyright owner and the other is for retention in the copyright owner's files if so desired.

Identifying the copyright holder can be a problem, particularly when purchasing software through a vendor. However, the problem is not insoluble and should be approached in a systematic manner. If the software itself does not have copyright information on the case, a general statement can usually be found at the end of the program as part of the credits. Identifying the copyright holder then becomes merely a matter of checking the cross referenced card files that are each set up alphabetically. One file is by title only and has only the source noted. The main file contains the title, producer and vendor with special notations for restrictions and/or permissions granted. A third file is an active vendor file only. Finally, a correspondence file contains a copy of the letters requesting special usage permission and the copyright owner's responses paired with the request.

The following should be considered in writing for permission.

1. The letter should specifically identify the items to be copied and the need, purpose, and use of the materials. Use letterhead stationery.

2. Set up master card index for each company containing:

    a. Date of permission or refusal.

    b. Work order number, if used.

    c. Amount charged, if any.

    d. Restrictions imposed by copyright owner.

3. Cross index by program title and company only.

4. Generate a printout listing usage by instructor name.

5. Maintain paper file of requests and the responses.

Maintaining An Information File

Some organizations believe that "no records are better." However, TCJC-NE believes that memories can fail, but records are useful – not only for the specific transaction, but also as a stimuli to help recall specific needs and discussions leading up to the actual requests. However, should questions ever arise about the legitimacy of copies made on campus, appropriate records provide evidence of good faith by the institution.

College records identify the following transactions between October, 1973 and February, 1987. Nine hundred and three special requests were sent to copyright holders. Of those requests eight hundred and ten were granted and only ninety three requests were denied. This is an 89.7% affirmative response.

Of those requests granted, 622 requests were granted with no charge. Of those having charges, the fee ranged from $.45 to $282.50. The median cost of charges was $50.81 for the one hundred and eighty eight requests granted with fee charges.

Types of Permission Requested

A variety of requests for permission occur and the reference staff must be conversant enough with the law to recognize when permissions are needed. Duplication rights are sometimes granted with a fee and sometimes free. When a fee is charged, a purchase order is sent. The following types of requests have been addressed by TCJC-NE with success.

1. Add a narration to a commercial slide presentation. Response was "feel free to add, delete, or adjust" because the copyright owner personally did not like "canned narratives."

2. Reproduce materials from a workbook. Granted on condition that material is limited to TCJC students on campus.

3. Dub a videotape. No charge since it was produced at another educational institution.

4. Change video format. Normally from U-matic to Beta on condition that the U-matic would be archived and not used.

5. Slides to filmstrip.

6. Divide a long program into subsections.

7. Audio cassette recording read from a text. Request was granted after determining that the company had no published audio tapes on the market.

Conclusion

C. Dan Echols, Dean of Learning Resources, at Tarrant County Junior College - Northeast, is a strong advocate of the utilization of instructional technology in the classroom. Equating copyright with income tax, something with which we are all familiar, his charge to the media staff is to see that "we get everything we are entitled to without taking that which is beyond the law." With this view of the copyright law as part of the legal system's effort to protect the original creations, the philosophy of TCJC-NE regarding copyright is quite healthy.

What it all comes down to is that the Media Center staff's responsibility is to support the faculty in its effort to provide the most effective, stimulating learning environment possible within the existing legal limitations. And isn't that what we are all trying to do? Again, this information is presented as ONE way to develop a system that meets the legal limitations while addressing the needs of an enthusiastic faculty dedicated to providing the best educational opportunities possible. Each institution must examine its staff, its curriculum and its approach to the copyright issue and proceed from there to develop the system that best meets its respective needs. However, we can all rest assured that a policy alone will not do the job that a policy and its appropriate applications will do.

BIBLIOGRAPHY

Becker, Gary, *New Copyright Law*, Part I. IT Services. Duval, P., 2037 N. Main, Jacksonville, FL 32206

Bender, Ivan, Regular Column in TLC (The Licensing Center).

Helm, Virginia, *Software Quality and Copyright: Issues in Computer Assisted Instruction.* Washington, D.C.; Association for Educational Communications and Technology., 1984.

Johnson, Beda, *How to Acquire Legal Copies of Video Programs.* San Diego; Video Resources Enterprise, 1986.

Official Fair-Use Guidelines: Complete Texts of Four Official Documents Arranged For Use By Educators, 3rd ed., Friday Harbor, WA; Copyright Information Services, 1987.

Miller, Jerome K. *Video/Copyright Seminar,* 1988. Friday Harbor, WA; Copyright Information Services, annual.

"Off-Air Copying Guidelines." *Instructional Innovator.* September, 1981.

Talab, R.S. *Commonsense Copyright: A Guide to New Technologies.* Jefferson, NC; McFarland, 1986.

Vlcek, Charles W. *Copyright Policy Development: A Resource Book for Educators.* Friday Harbor, WA: Copyright Information Services. 1987

Wessel, David. "Word from the Front in War Against Unauthorized Copying." *Wall Street Journal.* February 10, 1987, p.21.

Chapter 6 :

Some Do's And Don'ts For Off-Air Videotaping

by

LaVerne W. Miller

In an educational framework the recording, use, and retention of videotapes are activities for which there are a number of do's and don'ts. Because of copyright restrictions, if you are the responsible media person you will need to protect your school, your employer and technicians, as well as yourself, by knowing how to get permission to record, use, or retain programs videotaped off the air. Not are all situations alike, depending upon the producer, the distributor and your own objectives. Our purpose here is to provide a brief practical list of do's and don'ts which will be helpful — for the novice at off-air taping.

I. First, get acquainted with the federal guidelines for off-air videotaping which apply under the copyright law. This is not a new subject. Off-air videotaping has been a subject of discussion since 1979. With the expanding use of videocassette recorders and the ease of off-air taping, educators needed to know the limitations and restrictions in the copyright law. In 1979, Rep. Robert Kastenmeier (D-Wis.), chairperson of the House Subcommittee on Courts, Civil Liberties and Administration of Justice, appointed a negotiating committee of nineteen educators and proprietors to write the guidelines. The guidelines apply the"fair use"provision of the copyright law to recording, using, and retaining television programs in an educational setting. They were published in the *Congressional Record* of October 14, 1979 (pages E4750-E4752).

The guidelines appear to be remarkably clear.

1. The guidelines apply only to off-air recording by non-profit educational institutions, for use in instruction and not for entertainment.

2. A broadcast may be recorded off the air simultaneously with broadcast (including simultaneous cable retransmission) and retained by a non-profit educational institution for a period of forty-five calendar days after the date of recording. Upon the conclusion of such retention period, all off-air recordings *must* be erased or destroyed immediately."Broadcast programs"are television programs transmitted by television stations for reception by the general public without charge.

3. Off-air recordings may be used once by teachers in the course of relevant teaching activities, and repeated once when instructional reinforcement is necessary. The showings are limited to classrooms and similar places devoted to instruction in a single building, cluster or campus, as well as in the home of students receiving formalized home instruction. The showing must take place during the first ten consecutive school days in the forty-five day calendar day retention period."School days"are school session days — not counting weekends, holidays, vacations, examination periods, or other scheduled interruptions — within the forty-five-calendar-day retention period.

4. Off-air recordings may be made only at the request of and used by individual teachers. They may not be regularly recorded in anticipation of requests. No program may be recorded off the air more than once at the request of the same teacher, regardless of the number of times the program is broadcast.

5. A limited number of copies may be reproduced from each off-air recording to meet the legitimate needs of teachers under these guidelines. Each additional copy is subject to all the provisions governing the original recording.

6. After the first ten consecutive school days, off-air recordings may be used through the end of the forty-five-calendar-day retention period for evaluation purposes, (i.e., to determine whether or not to include the program in the curriculum). They may not be used for student exhibition or any other non-evaluation purpose without authorization.

7. Off-air recordings need not be used in their entirety, but the recorded programs may not be altered from their original content. The recordings may not be physically or electronically combined or merged to constitute teaching anthologies or compilations.

8. All copies of off-air recordings must include the copyright notice displayed on the program.

9. Educational institutions are expected to establish appropriate control procedures to maintain the integrity of these guidelines.

II. Suppose an instructor has seen a program announced in the morning paper or the weekly program guide and she wants to record it. When the teacher asks that the program be recorded, ask the questions you would ask for use of any other audiovisual material. What classroom instruction will it be used for? When and where? The objective may be to fit the program into a lesson immediately. (In this case, we hope that the instructor has thought of a way of integrating the subject matter into the course or lesson so that the students will see the relationship between the video and the other aspects of the course.) Assuming it is clear that such integration is possible and useful, the copy of the program may be used *one time only* under the conditions stated in the guidelines, but it must be used within ten school days. It must be erased within forty-five days. After the ten-day period has passed, the program can be used *only* for evaluation purposes, and cannot be shown to a class. If you want to retain the tape for future use, you must negotiate an agreement to do so.

The tape may be retained after the forty-five day period only with permission. There is, of course, always the faculty member who says, "Who will know?" ("that there is a violation of copyright" is the unspoken end of the question). "Who will *care* about it this one time?" The first answer, of course, is "*we* will know." That becomes a question of personal ethics. The other answer is that *"somebody* may care" — a parent, a student, a disgruntled worker — and if you do not get permission, you will have to face the consequences, which might be legal action. This *one* time should be *no* time.

III. Do get permission in writing. You may use a letter or a form which you design. Although it is highly unlikely that someone will want to use a program from commercial television, there are times when teachers may want to use parts of taped news or documentaries. To secure permission to use the program beyond the ten teaching day limit, contact the local station and find out what procedures you need to use to obtain permission to retain the piece and use it. The contact person may be the "services coordinator" but the title varies. When you call the program source, the receptionist often will not be able to answer your questions — she "just answers the phone" and is not responsible for being a storehouse of broadcast information — but she should be able to give you the name of the services coordinator, from whom you can get the producer's name or the procedural information you need.

You will frequently need to obtain permission from the program producer. Write to the person and make sure you get permission in a written response or on whatever kind of form your organization uses. You may need to indicate your purpose, how you will use the program, and for how long.

Other educational uses of off-air recordings include the analysis of television advertisements. There are several disciplines in which such analysis is applicable, in the development of visual literacy and analytical skills, for example, or in English, communication studies, consumer studies, or the social sciences. Again, if these examples are used through off-air taping, they should be erased within forty-five days or permission must be obtained for retention. In the permitted length of time, new commercials will appear anyway, so there may be no real reason for retention. To teach this kind of analysis the teacher should have the students practice some generic analytic principles, in any case. An alternative is renting a film of outstanding advertisements receiving the annual CLIO Awards. The material tends to become dated, but the analysis of advertising is still applicable in a generic sense.

Newscasts are also dated, even if they are of historical significance, and the objective in viewing them should be examined. If you really want to retain the piece, get permission. Repeat the same process as previously described, getting responses in writing.

Sometimes people forget that the bottom line in the communication business is not only profit but also protection of the creator whose energies have made the piece possible, and who earns a living through royalties...and royalties equal money.

IV. Many state PBS networks and individual stations have negotiated for the right of teachers to retain programs videotaped off PBS stations for an extended period — frequently for a year. Each state has different rights, but the common or generic principle involved is to get permission. Information about these special rights can be obtained from your local PBS station.

V. Determine what site restrictions may exist. There are some factors which must be considered if you are getting permission to use a videotape for more than one school in a system or for more than one campus in a multi-campus institution. The question to ask is whether or not the permission is restricted to one instructional site or to more, and whether copies can be made for additional sites in the system. In some cases the tape may be used only at the original site and rights may need to be purchased for use at other sites or some arrangements made with the distributor of the program. The requirements may be different for each program.

VI. Special exemptions are frequently available for courses offered for college credit. In some states, community colleges and the local PBS stations offer college credit by watching the television program, reading related texts, and taking tests. Many colleges arrange for the students to communicate by telephone or special seminars with an instructor, who is not the instructor pictured on the program. The instructor of record is a local instructor who can advise students and answer questions. She grades the tests and assigns grades. Participating colleges may record the programs off the air and use the tapes in a learning lab setting for students to view if the students have missed a broadcast or want to review the material before a test. After the end of the semester, the tapes are erased unless the college purchased the right to retain them.

VII. The guidelines state that educational institutions are expected to establish appropriate control procedures to maintain the integrity of these guidelines. Therefore, it is wise to formulate a set of procedures for requesting permission to use and retain programs videotaped off the air. The procedures should be based in the Kastenmeir guidelines. A written policy should be distributed to the faculty, so everybody knows what is required to tape, get permission and retain the programs.

Taping from cable broadcasts also come under the Kastenmeir guidelines. Programs transmitted by television stations without charge to the general public may be recorded. However, pay services, such as HBO and Cinemax do not fall under the guidelines.

Always maintain good records to keep school matters straight. Having looked at a number of recording agreements, I am reminded of an incident in which lawyer Ralph Nader gave a speech at our institution. We asked that it be recorded for future use and an historical record. He agreed to sign it if I altered the language and eliminated the whereas language of the institutional page-long form down to its simplest element, which was only one sentence free of jargon!

The simple forms from Gary Becker's book seem best suited to remind teachers or media staffers of the Kastenmeir guidelines. We have Mr. Becker's permission to attach them to this chapter.

VIII. Think carefully about whether or not you will permit the use of school equipment for a program taped at home and brought in by an instructor. Tapes made at home for use in a classroom are subject to the same"fair use"guidelines as though they had been taped at the school. Because the person who taped the program at home is subject to the same institutional constraints as someone who taped the program at school, the individual who recorded the program may not retain it indefinitely. He is now operating under the guidelines for education and not under the privilege for home videotaping for private performance.

Gary Becker in his excellent little volume, *The Copyright Game Resource Guide*, second edition, published by Gary Becker, 1986, gives the following advice. (page 18).

Several notes of caution, however. One of the requirements for institutional taping is that if the guidelines are implemented, that such taping be monitored in order to be in compliance. If your institution intends to permit a program taped at home to be brought into the classroom, it will need to develop a tracking system which guarantees compliance with the guidelines. Secondly, there are no court cases or legal guidelines indicating that home taping for school use actually is permissible, although the opinions cited earlier are highly respected. Thirdly, although not directly related to copyright, is the situation whereby inappropriate materials are taped off-air and shown before a class. Educational institutions that allow programs taped at home to be brought into the classroom need to follow the congressional (Kastenmeir's) committee guidelines and adhere to the institutions' own materials selection policies.

IX. If you have questions about the definition of in-classroom use, the American Library Association publication, *American Libraries,* February 1986, defines this function.

In-classroom performance of a copyrighted videotape is permissible under the following conditions:

1. The performance must be by instructors (including guest lecturers) or by pupils;

2. the performance is in connection with face-to-fact teaching activities;

3. the entire audience is involved in the teaching activity;

4. the entire audience is in the same room or same general area;

5. the teaching activities are conducted by a non-profit education institution;

6. the performance takes place in a classroom or similar place devoted to instruction, such as a school library, gym, auditorium or workshop; and

7. the videotape is lawfully made; the person responsible had no reason to believe that the videotape was unlawfully made.

X. It is also a good idea to get on the mailing list of distributors or producers of television educational materials. Sometimes they make special arrangements or have "sales" of programs which will be aired and which you might want to tape off the air. You can often purchase duplicating rights for a relatively low cost — usually for "the life of the tape". Getting on a mailing list is, of course, always risky — one can be inundated. However, it is worth a try.

XI. In this chapter I have tried briefly to point out some basic considerations involved in off-air taping and ways to approach getting permissions. There are a number of sources of information to which an individual may turn. One of the useful sources is the Television Licensing Center which gives free extensive and current information about off-air taping. (Toll free 800-323-4222; in Illinois, call collect 312-256-3200.) Its *TLC Guide* is very valuable. Another good source is the publications on copyright of the American Library Association Office of Copyright, Rights and Permissions. An inexpensive videotape called *Copyright* also deals with off-air videotaping and is published by the Association for Information Media and Equipment (AIME), 108 Wilmont Road, Deerfield, Illinois 60015.

OFF-AIR RECORDING STATEMENT

This tape was recorded _____ on_____
                     (by myself/at my request)   (date)

The 10th consecutive school day from the recording date is

_____.

(date)

I will not use this recording more than once in relevant teaching activities. I will not repeat it more than once for reinforcement.

The 45th day after the recording date will be_____
                            (date)

I understand that I may use this recording from the 11th to the 45th day for teacher evaluation only. It will not be used for student exhibition during this time unless authorization is obtained from the copyright holder.

_____ copies have been made of this recording. Each one bears a copy of this statement.

This recording (these recordings) will be _____
                            erased/destroyed
no later than the 45th day as indicated above.

Teacher Signature_____

Media Staff Signature_____

Video Copyright Permissions

Illustration 1: REQUEST FOR OFF-AIR TAPING

One of the requirements of the "Guidelines for Off-Air Recording of Broadcast Programming for Educational Purposes" (Congressional Record, October 14, 1981) is that records be maintained to assure that fair use criteria are followed for programs recorded. Therefore the following information is necessary to assure that the institution complies with the criteria. Please Complete all information known.

Requestors Name_____

School_____Department_____

Class_____

Signature_____

PROGRAM TO BE RECORDED AT SCHOOL

Title of Program to be Recorded_____

Station or Channel_____Time_____Length of Program_____

Date Recorded_____Date of Use_____

Erase Date_____Date erased_____

By_____
(Signature)

PROGRAM RECORDED AT HOME
(to Be Completed by Recorder and User)

Title of Program Recorded_____

Station or Channel_____Time_____Length of Program_____

Date Recorded_____By_____

Date Returned to Recorder_____By_____
(Signature)

Would you recommend this material   ____ Highly Recommended
    for purchase, lease or license?   ____ Recommended
                                            ____ Not Recommended
How many times would you use this program each year?_____
Comments:

- - Fair Use Guidelines on Back Side - -

OFF-AIR REQUESTS

Date Requested	Job #	Requester	Program Title/ Channel/Time/Length	Date Taped	Format	10-Day Period Ending	45-Day Period Ending	Disposition Licensed Date	Length	Cost	Erased Date

Video Copyright Permissions

Internal Request for Authorization
To Duplicate Copyrighted Material

Division of General Administration

TO: Date _____
Firm _____
Address _____
_____

FROM:

School/District _____

Department _____

Telephone _____

Person making request_____ Title _____

We are requesting authorization to duplicate the following copyrighted material:

Title _____

Author_____

Subject _____

Medium_____

Rationale _____

_____

Number of copies to be made: _____

Copy medium: _____

Use of copies: _____

Anticipated date of first use: _____

Distribution of copies:_____

. . . .

PRODUCER REPLY:

Permission: □ granted □ denied

Details/Restrictions: _____

_____

Signature _____

Title_____ Date _____

48

Chapter 7 :

The Television Licensing Center

by

Brenda Coto

The Television Licensing Center (TLC) was established in 1979 to provide a bridge between the legal rights of producers of broadcast programming and the instructional needs of educators and librarians.

During the 1970's, as more and more video duplication equipment became available in homes, schools, colleges, and public libraries, it was clear that a mechanism should be established to allow educators to record television programs off the air and retain them for educational use. It was obvious that a central agency was needed to provide legal access to broadcast programming. TLC became the first and only single-source clearinghouse for securing licenses to retain and use programs videotaped off the air.

TLC offers free membership to all educational institutions, including colleges, universities, intermediate/regional media centers, school districts, public and private schools, and public libraries. TLC member institutions receive a complimentary subscription to the monthly newsletter and free copyright information from the Video Copyright Reference Service. This service offers a question-and-answer service pertaining to legal aspects of videotaping off the air.

TLC acquires licenses from producers for specific programs and series. The programs are announced in the TLC newsletter in advance of the broadcast date. Educators and librarians videotape the programs when they are broadcast and use them in classrooms under the terms of the fair-use guidelines. [1] To use the program beyond the terms of the fair-use guidelines, it is only necessary to call TLC on its 800 number to license continued use of the programs. One-year and life-of-the-tape licenses are available. The license fees are less than the price of buying the prerecorded program. Once the license is signed, the copies may be used in classrooms, media centers, learning labs, libraries, and at home for study. All public performance rights have been cleared and the producers receive a royalty from TLC. As a result, educators and librarians have the assurance that they are legally protected to use programs videotaped off the air and licensed by TLC. Programs from BBC, NBC, Annenberg/CPB Project, National Film Board of Canada, Canadian Broadcasting Co., and many independent producers are available under TLC licenses. TLC also offers information about programs that may be videotaped off the air and used without a license. For further information about TLC, phone (800) 323-4222, Ex 332. (In Illinois call collect (312) 878-2600.)

---

1   "Guidelines for Off-Air Recording of Broadcast
      Programming for Educational Purposes," *Congressional
      Record,* Oct. 14, 1981, p. E4751.

Chapter 8 :

Video Use in the Ministry of First Church: A Case Study

by

Paula Morrow

This "case study" is a composite of actual experiences in several different church settings. First Church does not exist, and all individuals are completely fictional.

When old Carl Wilson died, his family approached Rev. Clayman about giving a sizable donation to the church in memory of their patriarch. Rev. Clayman didn't have to think very long.

"You know," he told them, "Carl lived a long time and saw a lot of changes in the world during his life. But he never wished for the "good old days." Carl was always fascinated by technology, always looking forward, always loved to have the latest "gadgets." And Carl was always interested in helping to spread the word of the Lord. Now, there's one way you could combine those two interests of Carl's. You could give a gift that would enhance the ministry of this church, and at the same time really tickle Carl's fancy for what's new." Rev. Clayman went on to tell the family his suggestion for a memorial to Carl, and the family members went home to confer. A few days later, a generous check arrived at the church, earmarked "Video Ministry".

Members of First Church had plenty of ideas for using their video equipment even before the shiny camera, VCR, and huge color console arrived. The education director ordered a copy of *Making the Most of Video in Religious Settings,*[1] and called the denomination headquarters to find out what resources were available from the national church. The choir director dreamed of videotaping musical productions with the junior and senior choirs, and making the tapes available to the congregation. The adult class decided to tape interesting TV programs to view and discuss. Youth group leaders envisioned using movies to increase attendance and stimulate discussions. The worship committee talked of creating videos to train acolytes, altar guild, and lay readers. Even the nursery supervisor breathed a sigh of pleasure at how much easier baby-sitting would be, with Bible-story cartoons to show the children during lengthy adult meetings.

The former Bride's Room, where dozens of maidens had dressed for their weddings, was renamed the Video Room. A polished plaque beside the door proudly proclaimed:

VIDEO MINISTRY

IN LOVING MEMORY OF

CARL JAMES WILSON

1909-1988

In the first rush of excitement about the new video ministry, no one gave a thought to the copyright law. That subject first came up casually, at a Sunday evening youth gathering. The senior high youth group had planned a lively volleyball game followed by pizza and fellowship, but a sudden rainstorm interrupted their outdoor activities. As they huddled in the church hall, dripping and laughing, someone exclaimed, "Let's get a video!" Several of the more adventurous teens headed for a nearby video rental store — accompanied by a youth group sponsor, who wanted to be sure their selection was suitable for discus-

1   Neufer Emswiler, Tom. *A Complete Guide to Making the Most of Video in Religious Settings.* Behavioral Images, 1985.

sion. The pizza arrived, only slightly soggy, and as the group gathered around *The Karate Kid*, the familiar copyright warning about "home use only" flashed on the screen.

"I wonder if we'll all go to jail," joked a girl through her pepperoni. Everyone laughed — but the words stayed with the sponsor who had rented the video. On Monday, she phoned Rev. Clayman, and hesitantly brought up the subject.

"We'll look into it," he promised, and enlisted Suzanne, the education director, to help him.

Suzanne found a chapter on copyright in the Neufer Emswiler[2] book, and was quite taken aback by what she read there.

"Evidently," she told Rev. Clayman, "it really wasn't legal for our youth group to watch *The Karate Kid* here when their volleyball game was rained out."

"You're kidding!" Rev. Clayman exclaimed. "What's illegal about a church youth meeting?"

"According to this book, we had to have permission from the copyright owner for a public performance. And "public performance" is anything beyond a close circle of family and friends at home — even if it's free and just for a club meeting or a church social or something like that," Suzanne replied.

"Does that mean we can't use our new video equipment with the youth group or the couples club or the Sunday School after all?" asked Rev. Clayman in disbelief.

"Well, we can still use things from the video library at denominational headquarters," Suzanne said. "But I don't know about movies that were first made to be shown in theaters. I have some literature from a couple of church video clubs and other sources, and I've noticed that they offer some of the same titles we can rent locally. Let me call and see what kind of rights they offer."

---

2   *Ibid.*

53

The sales representative at the first video club Suzanne called was very encouraging. "You rent the videos from us for one month," she explained, "and they're yours to use any way you want to, just so they're not damaged."

"Well, I've noticed that we can rent some of the same titles locally, the Walt Disney films, for example. But they have a copyright notice that says they're for home use only," said Suzanne. "As I understand it, that means we can't use them for things like youth group meetings, because that's considered a public performance."

"Public performance is that you would pay to get in," stated the sales representative confidently. "Showing the video to your church group, that's not public, if you don't charge admission."

"So when we rent from you, we're getting a different kind of license?" Suzanne persisted.

The sales representative responded a bit testily. "When we purchase the films from Walt Disney and the other companies, they know what we're doing with them. They know we're a video rental club for churches. Churches are not going to make a profit. They're trying to show entertainment for their kids. They're trying to show education. So, do you want to enroll your church as a member?"

"I guess not, right now," said Suzanne. "I'll have to talk to our minister. But thanks for the information."

Suzanne called several other video rental places with similar results. Most of the clerks seemed uninformed about copyright; a few were defensive. Several of them offered the opinion that a performance wasn't "public" unless admission was charged. Suzanne, remembering what she had read, was not convinced.

It wasn't long before two mothers approached Suzanne about starting an "active parenting" series at the church. A friend of theirs from another congregation had highly recommended a series of educational videotapes by Dr. James Dobson, and they were interested in having a parents' discussion group that would meet on a weekday evening. Suzanne promised to find out about the tapes, and called the other church for information. Soon she had addresses to write for several catalogs of educational and religious videos. These tapes, she discovered, were sold with "audio-visual rights" (also known as "non-theatrical public performance rights"), which meant they could be used in a church setting as long as no admission was charges.

Suzanne also learned that the neighbor church owned two sets of tapes, which they had used quite successfully, and was interested in buying others.

"Let our church buy a set that you don't have," offered Suzanne. "Then we can trade back and forth, and have twice as many resources available."

One afternoon Katie, the youth group advisor, arrived at the church with a handful of brochures.

"I stopped by the public library to see what videos they have available," she explained, "and mentioned that I was from a church. I told the librarian about renting *The Karate Kid* for our youth group and then finding out it was illegal. She had a whole file on copyright, and let me borrow these brochures. Some of them tell about different kinds of licensing agreements."

Katie left the materials for Suzanne to read. Several of them included toll-free phone numbers, and Suzanne was soon on the phone.

The first place she called was MPLC — Motion Picture Licensing Corporation, in Stamford, Connecticut[3]. This, she learned, is a "blanket" licensing agency. Rather than getting permission to use a specific title on a specific date, the church could obtain an umbrella license to use all the movies they wanted throughout the year. The church would estimate their anticipated frequency of performances and size of audience, and a mutually agreeable fee would be negotiated. MPLC would send the church a simple contract to sign, and the church would then receive a "certificate of license" to use home videos.

---

[3]   Motion Picture Licensing Corporation, P.O. Box 3838, 2777 Summer Street, Stamford, CT 06905-0838; 1-800-338-3870; 203-353-1600.

"It's a great deal," Suzanne told Rev. Clayman as soon as she got off the phone. "The fee they offered me is less than twenty-five cents per person. And the best part is, we can just go down to the video rental store and rent videos whenever we want to. So we can still have the freedom to run out and pick something at the last minute, like the youth group did."

"Sounds good," said Rev. Clayman. "Can we rent anything in the whole store?"

"Well, no," admitted Suzanne. "MPLC gives us rights to just certain studios. But they have all of Walt Disney, Touchstone, MGM/United Artists, most of the things we'd be wanting. And they said they're negotiating with other studios, so they'll have more and more available as time goes on."

"Do you recommend we go with it?" asked Rev. Clayman.

"I think so," said Suzanne. "Then we'll know we're legal, at least about the movies."

Meanwhile, Joanne, the Sunday School superintendent, had also been busy talking with her friends at other churches. Everyone was enthusiastic about using video in the classroom.

"If you're shy on volunteers, the videos are a great way to get people in there," one Sunday School leader told her. "Don't ask people to be teachers, call them "monitors." They just push buttons—turn tapes on and off, and serve as discussion leaders."

Joanne discovered that there was no shortage of material available, especially for an adult class. Besides the regular course-type videos she could rent or purchase from catalogs or borrow from other churches, there were interesting programs on local and network TV.

"It's a good way to inexpensively have subject matter," another friend confided. "Just tape it at home and bring it to Sunday School."

After consulting with Suzanne and Rev. Clayman, Joanne set up a regular Sunday morning adult class using video. Together, they set up procedures that they felt would keep them within the copyright law.

Two interested church members were recruited to be the "leaders" for the class. Using money from the "Sunday School curriculum" item in the budget, the church subscribed to Cultural Information Service[4], which offers previews of upcoming TV programs, movies, videos, and paperback books. Joanne also got a copy of the local ITV (instructional television) schedule by calling the public broadcasting station in town. Using these two resources, plus TV Guide and word of mouth, the leaders selected programs they thought would be worth using in class. Usually they could set up a tentative schedule two months in advance, with flexibility for changes depending upon local programming or class requests.

Since the church VCR had a programmable timer, it was a simple matter to set it each Sunday to automatically tape the programs they wanted during the coming week. The class leaders would either watch the programs at home as they were aired or preview the church's tapes to be sure they wanted to used them, and to make up a few discussion-starting questions.

Under the copyright law, the tapes could only be used in the first ten "teaching days." The church had to either erase these off-air tapes after forty-five days or else get permission to keep them longer. Usually the class would use a tape once, then erase it. Since the tapes were being used in a systematic course of instruction, the church felt comfortable about their use being legal.

Sometimes, the class wanted to keep a copy of a tape after they had used it. In these cases, Suzanne called the local station for rights information. Some ITV programs automatically allowed repeated use for one school year, and the public broadcasting station could give Suzanne that information on the spot. For other educational programs, and for commercial programs, the station would give her the address and phone number of the copyright holder. It cost the church a few long distance phone calls, but Suzanne was usually able to reach someone who had the authority to give her permission to keep the tape. She would identify herself, the church, and the tape she wanted to keep, explaining how it would be used. After receiving verbal permission,

---

4   Cultural Information Service, P.O. Box 786, Madison Square Station, New York, NY 10159.

Suzanne would ask if she could send a confirmation letter for the person to sign and return to her for the church files.

Suzanne worked up a simple form letter which she would adapt to fit each particular case. (The letter appears in Appendix A.)

The letter was personalized to fit the exact agreement reached by phone, and individually typed on church letterhead. Some companies were glad to give permission; other insisted on strict time limits or other restrictions, which were reflected in the letter.

Sometimes Suzanne was not able to obtain free permission to keep a tape. Then she, the class leaders, and Rev. Clayman would have to decide just how badly they wanted to keep that particular tape. First Church joined, at no cost, the Television Licensing Center[5], a clearinghouse for off-air videotaping rights. From this center, they could purchase a license to keep and use any off-air tape. The licensing fee was usually in the neighborhood of $50 per program for one year of use, or $125 for "life of tape" use.

If Suzanne and her colleagues felt the program was not worth the $50, Suzanne would simply erase that tape. In a few cases, one specific individual in the class had asked to have a tape kept, and Suzanne would give the tape to that person privately, for home use only.

As interest in video grew at First Church, more and more members made suggestions for its use. One day a parishioner came to see Rev. Clayman.

"I've been transferred," he told the minister, "and we'll be moving out of state this summer. We've decided we'd like to donate our satellite dish to the church, if you're interested."

---

5   Television Licensing Center, 5547 N. Ravenswood Avenue,
     Chicago, IL 60640-1199; 800-323-4222; In Illinois (collect)
     312-878-2600.

"Of course!" exclaimed Rev. Clayman. Soon Suzanne had a new area to investigate.

Having the satellite dish allowed the church to receive many more networks than were available through the local cable company. The librarian at the public library—who by now knew Suzanne quite well—supplied a list of satellite programming channels with names, addresses, and phone numbers of contact persons.[6] A number of these were specifically religious networks, and Suzanne was pleasantly surprised when she began calling them for information.

"Our programs are free," she was told again and again. "As long as it's for church use and you're not selling them or charging admission, we're happy to have you using them."

Other satellite networks were commercial, and Suzanne found that the permissions procedures she had worked out for television stations applied to the satellite programs as well.

"These permissions really are a nuisance," Suzanne sighed on morning, after a frustrating hour on the phone trying to reach the person who could give her permission to keep a tape the adult class had found particularly stimulating. "Why can't we just keep the tape and keep our mouths shut? It's not like we were trying to put NBC out of business!"

Rev. Clayman glanced up, a twinkle in his eye. "You don't really mean that, Suzanne," he said. "You're an honest person, and you wouldn't feel right about doing something illegal, even if nobody knew."

"Well, you're right," Suzanne admitted. "But it's still a nuisance!"

"I know that, and I appreciate your taking the time and trouble to follow through with it," Rev. Clayman replied. "Because, Suzanne,

---

6   Vlcek, Charles W. *Copyright Policy Development.* Copyright Information Services, 1987. Apopendix II-E. Satellite Programming Directory, pp. 112-128.

your actions are a witness to your beliefs. Remember what Jesus said to His disciples: 'He who is faithful in a very little is faithful also in much, and he who is dishonest in a very little is dishonest also in much.' If we're going to preach the Gospel here, let's be faithful even about something as seemingly little as one half-hour videotape."

"Amen!" responded Suzanne with a grin, picking up the phone once more.

Appendix A

SAMPLE LETTER

Dear (name of person she had talked to):

Thank you for talking with me on (date). As I explained in our phone conversation, First Church would like permission to retain one videotaped copy of (name or identify program) for a period of _____. We will use this tape for (specific purpose) and will not charge an admission or other fee of any kind.

We will also make this tape available to members of our church to borrow and watch at home. Again, there will be no fee or service charge.

I'm enclosing two copies of this letter to confirm the verbal permission you gave me by phone. Please sign the bottom of one copy and return it in the enclosed stamped, addressed envelope. The other copy is for your files.

Thank you again for your time and for your assistance to the educational ministry of First Church.

In peace,

Suzanne Anderson

Director, Christian Educ.

Appendix B

SOURCES OF PUBLIC PERFORMANCE VIDEO

Dynamic Audio Visuals
24005 West 95th
Shawnee Mission, KS 66227
(913) 764-3206

Distributing agency for public performance, educational, and home use videos. The catalog of titles clearly states the specific rights for each item.

EcuFilm and Video
810 - 12th Avenue South
Nashville, TN 37203
(800) 251-4091

Distributing agency for nine cooperating groups and denominations including United Methodist Church, Disciples of Christ, United Church of Christ, the Episcopal Church, Lutheran Church in America, the Presbyterian Church, the National Council of Churches, World Council of Churches, and Mirano Missionaries, a Catholic group. Over 1,000 titles are available on either a rental or purchase basis. All may be used for public performance.

Alternate View Network
Head of Texas St.
P.O. Drawer 1567
Shreveport, LA 71165

Educational and religious programming focusing on ethical and related issues, available on satellite Galaxy 1. Programs may be taped for non-profit use in churches.

Trinity Broadcasting Network
P.O. Box A
Santa Ana, CA 92711

Family Christian programming, available on satellite SATCOM F3. Programs may be taped for non-profit use in churches.

Chapter 9 :

Copying Free

by

Jerome K. Miller

Some television programs may be videotaped off the air and used without a license. These are usually public domain programs or copyrighted programs that have been cleared for duplication and use by nonprofit agencies.

Public Domain Programs

Programs in the public domain are not protected under the US copyright act. At one time, many producers were careless about protecting their copyrights and many programs fell into the public domain. That is no longer true. Today, the only television programs that are in the public domain are programs produced by the federal government, which are not eligible for copyright protection. These include (1) presidential addresses, (2) hearings conducted by the Senate and House of Representatives, and (3) debates from the floor of the House of Representatives. (If the Senate permits its debates to be broadcast, they also will be in the public domain.)

Televised addresses by governors and state legislative bodies are probably copyrighted. However, a few letters to the governor and the president of each legislative body should be sufficient to have the programs cleared for duplication and use by nonprofit agencies within the state. (That is a small favor to ask of a politician.)

Cleared Programs

Copyrighted programs which are cleared for free duplication and use fall into two categories: A. selected programs broadcast by nonprofit television stations, and B. selected programs broadcast by commercial television stations.

Most of the cleared programs are broadcast by stations affiliated with the Public Broadcasting Service (PBS). The clearance for PBS programs varies from state to state, and sometimes from station to station within a state. Many PBS programs are funded by a consortium of stations and state educational agencies. The consortium that funds program development receives broadcast rights for the program as well as extended-use rights for nonprofit agencies in their viewing areas. The terms of the agreement vary from program to program, but they typically permit nonprofit agencies to videotape the programs off the air and to show them as often as needed for one year. This permission is granted free of charge. Information about programs cleared for duplication and use in your area may be obtained from the educational coordinator or public service coordinator at the local PBS station.

The extended-use rights available from one station may not be available from a nearby station. The stations and state agencies cannot afford to participate in all the available program consortia, so they cannot clear every program for their viewers. Nonprofit agencies that receive PBS programs from more than one station may be able to secure extended-use rights from one station that are not available from another station.

If a program was not cleared for extended use in your viewing area, the rights may be available for a modest fee from PBS Video, 1320 Braddock Pl., Alexandria, VA 22314-1698. Life-of-the tape licenses for programs videotaped off the air are $100 for thirty-minute programs, $125 for sixty-minute programs, and $150 for longer programs.

Commercial television stations and the commercial networks rarely offer permission for extended-use of network programs.

However, most stations readily grant permission to duplicate and use locally-produced programs.

A few important documentary programs broadcast on the commercial networks are cleared in advance for duplication and use by schools and other nonprofit agencies, when the licensing fee was paid in advance by a major commercial firm. In recent years, the "National Geographic Specials" have been cleared for school use by a major oil company. Information about copying and using the "National Geographic Specials" may be obtained from National Geographic Society, 17th. & M Sts., NW, Washington, DC 20036. Information about free duplication and use of other commercial programs may be obtained from the Television Licensing Center (TLC). This information regularly appears in the TLC newsletter.

Part III :

Case Studies

Chapter 10 :

Videotaping Off Satellites

by

Marvin A. Davis

Satellites offer almost unlimited expansion of the communication capabilities throughout the world. Satellites operate under regulations issued by the Federal Communications Commission (F.C.C.), as are other communication systems such as telephone, telegraph, microwave, etc. The satellites themselves provide the capability for point-to-point communication. Multiple-point or large-area coverage can be specified by the person sending the communication. Materials sent via satellite include unedited newscasts, computer-readable data telephone conversations, and military communications. The variety of content is almost unlimited and the receiving sites can be worldwide.

The usefulness of satellite transmissions to educators seems open ended, limited only by the imagination of the person who has the equipment to receive it. However, the utilization of satellite transmissions is under strict regulation by the F.C.C. and by contracts between the transmitting and receiving agencies.

In general, earth stations are under contract and receive satellite transmissions for specific purpose. For example, a public television station, which is a member of PBS, receives the "feed" for over-the-air broadcasting. PBS associate member educational institutions covered by state contract also may receive the program "feed".

Authorized receiving agencies pay a membership fee to receive the program "feed." In addition, they frequently pay the producer for the programs they retransmit. These contracts give the producers the income to continue operations. the loss of income from unauthorized receptions has prompted many organizations to scramble their materials so they cannot be viewed by non-member agencies.

The organization sending the programs via satellite cannot often provide copying and performance rights to other users, since they only own the broadcast and cable transmission rights. Many distributors are not interested in helping educators obtain rights, because it does not provide income for them. Quite often the transmitting organization obtains programs from various sources with the right to transmit them via satellite to the members of the transmitting organization. As such, the transmitting organization does not have the rights to duplicate or use the programs in education. The transmitting organization may not know where to obtain the rights, as they may only be acquainted with agencies that sell satellite transmission rights. Quite often, the sources for the two releases are different.

At best, it becomes very difficult to obtain rights to many of the programs which are available via satellite and which may have uses in education. If so, why not use them and not worry about copyright or communication laws? That is no different than stealing anything else. The laws that protect satellite communication also protect your telephone conversations. Organizations transmitting materials by satellite have their right to privacy and security.

In general, the procedure to obtain the rights is to contact the transmitting organization. If you are fortunate, the transmitting organization does own the rights, and can provide them to you. If they do not control the rights, they may be able to provide you with the companies, addresses and phone numbers of the distributors or organizations that control the rights.

You must contact each agency individually to obtain rights. Even at this point they may not be able to provide the educational rights because they may simply be distributors. You may have to go one step further — to the original owner or producer to obtain these rights.

In general, it is a long process requiring several weeks. Often the schedules for the various transmissions of materials are not provided far enough in advance to secure the rights prior to satellite transmission. It does, however, provide educators the opportunity to view materials and thus determine whether they are worth the effort to search for rights for utilization in education

The materials which are easiest to obtain rights to are the unedited portions of newscasts. If you contact the news company directly, stating the reasons and the intent of use, you may be able to obtain rights to use these materials within your organization.

There are also educational agencies, either state or private, which offer satellite recording rights. TI-IN, Utah State, and several Canadian agencies sell rights for either inservice or for classroom utilization, or they may provide you with the opportunity to become a member of their organization.

In summary, most satellite organizations cannot authorize new uses of the materials and they often do not know what is needed or where to obtain rights. The materials they are transmitting come from various sources and therefore require multiple agreements and clearances. Since the transmitting agency will, in general, not gain from these agreements, they often are very slow in responding or unwilling or unable to provide the information.

Many of these agencies are members of other organizations, such as PBS. They pay a fee to receive programs, which are separate from the charges for rights. Therefore, if you are not a member, they would say that it is illegal for you to receive their materials. To secure these rights, you must find a way to become a part of the system. This can either be a full member or part of an existing membership, such as an associate member of a state broadcasting system.

A satellite reception antenna can greatly increase the educational opportunities, but it does not necessarily decrease the cost. In fact, as more programs are available via satellite it may greatly increase the costs because programs produced for satellite transmission may have a very high price tag. Your choice is to pay or not use — not to steal. The need does not justify the mean.

71

Chapter 11 :

Three Permissions Surveys

by

Mary Jo James

INTRODUCTION

Directing a media program requires a working knowledge of the very complex copyright law. In order to negotiate appropriate media agreements, media users must know their rights as well as the restrictions imposed by various producers. The best means for acquiring the necessary background information is through study of the law itself, producers' catalogs, and current literature. In addition, it is important to examine the physical property itself. A tape, case, or label may contain restrictions. Some companies now extend formal licensing agreements prior to filling a purchase order. Each purchaser needs to understand rights and then to ask for the additional rights needed, specifying acceptable conditions of use. Producers and distributors appreciate working with users who understand marketing problems; they are accustomed to compromise. Such discussions generally result in better agreements for both parties.

Legal counsel for the Tennessee State Board of Regents, the governing board for the twenty universities, community colleges, and technical institutes in Tennessee, studied the copyright issue. Because the institutions had entered into a Media Consortium in 1978, the Regents advised that we approach the issue with caution. During late 1984 and 1985, to clarify users' rights and restrictions, three surveys were undertaken by the Executive Director of the Media Consortium at the request of legal counsel. Because individual conditions and circumstances have influenced the responses, no companies are mentioned by name in the surveys which follow.

I.   CLOSED-CIRCUIT SURVEY

The Consortium is on the mailing list for approximately 150 companies. In 1984, their most current catalogs were examined for restrictive policy statements. Any statements which might prohibit members of the Media Consortium from using purchased materials over closed-circuit campus cable television systems were noted. Fifty of the 150 catalogs stated limitations which, without further clarification, would deny use over campus TV system. In their use of terminology such as "televised," "electronic transmission," "conventional playback use within a single-building," and "exhibition to viewers not in immediate presence," producers effectively refused use of the major media-delivery systems available to members of the Media Consortium. Most of the catalogs required a purchaser of their materials to define the extent of the closed-circuit system prior to use.

Logic indicated that most sellers probably would permit use over single-campus, closed-circuit underground cable systems. It was felt that companies would not interpret as threatening any system which neither broadcasts over airwaves, advertises its cabled programs, nor exhibits to anyone other than faculty and students for instructional purposes. There appeared to be primarily a communication problem.

Because we own materials listed in the catalogs of thirty of the fifty companies, a letter was sent to those thirty companies. The restrictive statement from the company catalog was quoted, and the closed-circuit delivery system used by the schools was described in detail. The letter requested agreement to our playing any programs purchased from the company over our transmission systems. A place was provided at the bottom of the letter for a signature, title, and date. Request was made for the appropriate person to sign and return the letter to the Executive Director. If consent was not to be given, the letter asked to discuss the matter.

Whenever possible, each letter was individualized and mailed to the attention of the direct sales representative or regional manager with whom business was normally conducted. Letters also were sent to marketing directors of those companies which do not use direct sales persons. As expected, letters addressed to the former group generally received a prompt and favorable response. The response rate for the latter group was poor. In some cases, in order to obtain reply, second letters were written to the president of the company and marked "second request." Even so, 23% failed to respond.

DISTRIBUTION OF RESPONSES

21	yes	70%
02	yes, with additional fees	07%
07	no response	23%
30		100%

A number of the persons with whom the Executive Director interacted simply did not have a clear idea of the technology or terminology of cable transmission. Those persons having the least contact with the ultimate user-purchaser, such as legal counsel, were least likely to understand campus closed-circuit systems and were reluctant to agree.

Although we had hoped for a 100% agreement, the survey and its results contained few surprises. Eventually twenty-one of the thirty companies consented. Two more consented to the use of their materials only if additional fees were paid. We declined the option to pay those additional fees and will merely restrict their programs from use over cable. These restrictions are bound to affect our future purchases. We acknowledge a company's right to restrict but there is a cost, in terms of sales.

We feel that we should no longer purchase from those seven companies which failed to respond. Legal counsel advised that, with respect to materials already owned, our efforts showed good faith and further action was not recommended. If we have interest in any of their products in the future, we will relate our request to play over closed-circuit to a specific purchase; hopefully this will re-open communication on the issue.

In light of the possibility for legal action in current relationships between media producers and users, if you have a cable system, it seems advisable that you read your catalogs carefully. Like us, you may want a company to "put it in writing."

SAMPLE LETTER

COMPANY

Dear (It is preferable to direct the letter to an individual; if not possible, write to the vice president of marketing, director of sales, etc.)

A study has been made of educational media catalogs for statements related to the use of video programs over closed-circuit television systems. Your catalog contains one or more statements which we feel require further clarification. We either own some of your programs or anticipate previewing and purchasing from you; therefore, your written response is important to us.

Video programs which this University purchases are played over a very restricted, single-campus, closed-circuit system. The origination point of this system is in a Learning Lab, the University's audio-visual library. Via underground cable, we program to about twelve classrooms; no dormitories, cafeterias, or recreational facilities can access any program shown over the system. Programs are shown, at the request of the teacher for one class at a time. The alternative to using the system is for a teacher to walk across campus and to check out the tape and equipment. Frequently equipment to play back is not available. Students may view programs in the Lab in individual carrels, and this utilizes the same system.

We would like your permission to play programs purchased from you over the system described above. If you cannot respond to this inquiry, please forward this letter to the appropriate person. We look forward to hearing from someone in your company.

Thank you for your assistance.

Sincerely,

Title

II. PUBLIC PERFORMANCE RIGHTS SURVEY

Infringement occurs if a copyrighted work is publicly performed, without authorization of the copyright owner. Under the "first sale" doctrine, the purchase of a particular copy of a work permits the purchaser to rent or otherwise distribute that copy, but it does not authorize a public performance. The copyright owner retains that exclusive right.

The terms "perform" and "perform—a work 'publicly'" are defined in U.S. Copyright Law Section 110. The definition of "perform" in relation to a motion picture or other audiovisual work means merely to display the images or to play the soundtrack. A performance, therefore, is considered private when it occurs within a home (or dormitory room) with only the normal circle of a family and its social acquaintances present. A public performance occurs at any place which is open to the public or in which people outside the family circle and its social acquaintances are gathered. Location and the composition of the audience are the determining factors. Restricting the performance to only students is not limited enough, in terms of "social acquaintances," to avoid infringement.

The only exception which allows for a lawful public performance is defined in Section 110(1). Requirements for the exemption are that the performance: 1) take place in the course of face-to-face teaching; 2) be given by an instructor or pupil; 3) take place in a nonprofit educational institution; and 4) take place in a classroom or similar place devoted to instruction. Also, the copy must be "lawfully made."

Obviously, public libraries do not qualify for the exemption. School libraries may or may not qualify. To be safe, it is recommended that the classroom teacher accompany students to the library. Librarians can be held accountable if misuse of library-owned materials occurs, and this can easily occur through traditional in-house library usage or when materials are checked out to patrons. Our legal counsel has advised us, in the absence of clear permissive statements in media catalogs, that we technically violate copyright law when we permit use of tapes in library carrels.

In June, 1985, a letter was mailed to the ninety-nine companies from which we were buying or had bought AV materials. The letter requested written permission: 1) to display products legally-acquired from them in our library carrels to students and faculty for instruction, hobby or interest use; and 2) to check out the material to faculty for their instructional purposes. The letter requested a signature at the bottom of the page if permission was granted.

Sixty-two of the ninety-nine companies acknowledged, without any qualifier, our right to use their titles. One reserved rights for certain programs; six denied permission; and twenty-eight did not respond, even to a second letter. Finally, two responses were irrelevant.

	DISTRIBUTION OF RESPONSES	
62	yes	63%
01	reserved rights, certain prog.	01%
06	no	06%
28	no response	28%
02	irrelevant response	02%
99	total	100%

Fifty-three of the sixty-two who gave permission were our regular educational sources; they understood our needs and expected us to use media as described. Eight of the ninety-nine firms marketed primarily to businesses rather than to educational institutions; five of these eight eventually conceded to our request. Fourteen of the ninety-nine were half-inch distributors, and four of these were among those who gave permission for use in carrels and check-out to faculty.

DISTRIBUTION OF FAVORABLE RESPONSES		
53	educational	85%
05	business-oriented	08%
04	half-inch	06%
62	companies granted perm.	100%

Some of the responses from the half-inch distributors were rather interesting and frequently were difficult to interpret. One company gave permission, erroneously quoting the "first sale" concept as authority. Another indicated that it would be necessary to discuss titles individually, clearing them one by one. It became obvious that permission would be given for materials in public domain and for very little else. Permission to use media in carrels was denied by five half-inch video companies, two of which stated that, since they did not own copyrights, they could not legally grant permission. One offered to sell a license agreement. Four, or more than one-third, of the half-inch companies failed to respond to the letter. An outright denial definitely turns off a prospective customer. It should be noted that no response to a copyright-conscious person has the same effect as a rejection.

Problems will continue to surface if educational institutions purchase materials from certain half-inch video distributors and from many business-oriented firms, expecting to use them in library carrels and viewing rooms. ducational, business, and home media markets do not mix well. The latter two may send their catalogs to us, but if they are only distributors, they cannot legally give the public performance rights which belong to the producer/copyright holder.

It is hoped that as educational, business-oriented, and half-inch video companies print new catalogs, they will include statements which will address the public performance issue.

SAMPLE LETTER

Dear (It is preferable to direct the letter to an individual; if not possible, write to the vice president of marketing, director of sales, etc.)

There has been considerable discussion among media specialists with regard to interpretation of various elements of copyright law. This letter is written in an attempt to clarify our rights to use audiovisual materials purchased or licensed from your company.

The copyright law, Section 110.1, seems to clearly permit the showing of any and all legally-owned audiovisual material in a classroom as long as it is part of a "face-to-face" teaching activity. A very few media catalogs make a statement with regard to public performances. According to our State Board of Regents legal counsel, clarification should be obtained from media producers with respect to where and to whom a motion picture or videocassette may legally be exhibited, other than "face-to-face," with a teacher before a class. We need to be assured that we are permitted to extend the learning activity involving films into a library, learning lab, carrel, etc.

For example, if a student is absent from the "face-to-face" instruction and is assigned to view a film/tape in a carrel, housed in a library/lab, we consider this a legitimate use of your material. Also, we believe you will agree that students should be permitted to request the use of material simply because they have an interest in a topic.

You may respond by acknowledging your agreement to our above assumptions on the bottom of this letter. If we do not hear from you within thirty days, we will assume that you have no objections. Please advise us to the contrary, with specifics, should you disagree.

Sincerely,

Title

The use of our audiovisual materials as described above is permitted.

_____   _____
Signed   Title

Date:_____

81

III. TRAINING MEDIA DISTRIBUTORS ASSOCIATION SURVEY

As the name implies, the Training Media Distributors Association (TMDA) is an association of producers of training materials. Its forty-two regular and associate members are listed in a small booklet, *Imagine A World Without,* which TMDA distributed in early 1985. It is available from the association, 5000 Van Nuys Boulevard, Sherman Oaks, CA 91403. These association members send catalogs to educational institutions; although educators do purchase from them, their primary market is industry.

Since the Media Consortium does business with seventeen of the firms listed in the booklet, we read with particular interest a Special Notice on the inside of the back cover. The notice offers a reward of up to $5,000 for information "leading to the arrest and conviction or successful prosecution of any training or videotape pirate," along with several ominous statements. While we do not believe we have been guilty of piracy, such a written notice does put the reader on guard, and the booklet was made a discussion item on the agenda of the May 1985 Media Consortium meeting.

Page four of the booklet lists "Some Things to Avoid":

1. Copying or duplicating films, videotapes, or related printed material.

2. Broadcast of programs over open or closed-circuit television systems.

3. Charging an admission fee or unauthorized public performance, such as use in an advertised seminar.

4. Subdistribution for rental or free loan outside of the customer's organization.

5. Use of preview prints for training purposes rather than professional evaluation.

Of the five restrictions, numbers three and four were of most concern to us since the closed-circuit survey was already in process. The wording of number three had the potential of restricting the use of materials by certain higher education programs, such as continuing education. Discussion indicated that the continuing education programs which were on our campuses used audiovisual materials and that they advertised classes for which fees were charged. Since AV materials were incidental to their classes, films and tapes were not part of their advertisements. The four technical institutes felt that number four also required some clarification. The mission of our technical institutes involves working with local industry, and specially-arranged classes are conducted by them for businesses. These classes are generally taught by regular institute instructors but are sometimes conducted off-campus. The relationship between the institutes and local businesses might be a problem under both items three and four.

Each of the twenty media collections is operated independently, with no interlibrary loan or rental to each other or to other institutions, businesses, or agencies. Entire training packages have never been acquired from these TMDA companies. Generally regular faculty, not adjunct faculty, teach the courses, and we felt that it would be difficult for us to monitor their use of AV materials with regard to kinds of classes an instructor is teaching.

In June, at the request of our legal counsel, letters were sent to seventeen TMDA members requesting permission to use any materials purchased from them in our continuing education courses and with other institutional activities. The letters specified that such activities were sometimes held off-campus.

Fifteen responses were received. Ten companies agreed to the use as proposed in the letter. Two more companies permitted us to use their materials with continuing education courses, but other instructional activities had to be held on the campus. One company flatly denied our use. Instead of answering the questions, two additional companies responded by sending contracts which have been interpreted as denials.

Needless to say, these responses have affected our preview and purchase practices. Materials previously purchased from companies which have not lifted the restrictions for our campuses have been identified and labeled. Continuing education faculty have been advised of the restrictions.

DISTRIBUTION OF RESPONSES

10	yes	59%
02	conditional	12%
03	no	17%
<u>02</u>	no response	<u>12%</u>
17		100%

SAMPLE LETTER

COMPANY

Dear (It is preferable to direct the letter to an individual; if not possible, write to the vice president of marketing, director of sales, etc.)

(Company) is listed in the Training Media Distributors Association pamphlet, A WORLD WITHOUT FILM AND VIDEO PROGRAMS. This pamphlet has been carefully read, noting that your association aggressively advertises a reward for information leading to the "arrest and conviction or successful prosecution of a film or videotape pirate."

We do not believe we are in violation of the prohibitions contained in the pamphlet; this letter is written to obtain an interpretation of item one under "Some Things To Avoid."

We would like your permission to use programs purchased from your company for all teaching activities. This would include use in our on-campus continuing education classes. Regular faculty teach these classes, and the use of audiovisual materials is incidental to their instruction. Fees are charged for the classes, and while the classes themselves are advertised, the materials never are. The university does not rent or lend its materials to outside organizations. Faculty may use the materials only on campus, and students use video materials only in the Learning Lab, the audiovisual library.

We do not want to jeopardize our relationship with any company with which we do business. It is important that we identify and take advantage of all rights permitted us with regard to future purchases, as well as to proceed cautiously in the use of materials we already own. Your response will assist us in making good decisions.

If you cannot respond to this inquiry, please forward this letter to the appropriate person. We look forward to hearing from someone in your company.

Sincerely yours,

Title

Appendix

TMDA Regular Members

Advanced Systems, Inc.
American Media, Inc.
BNA Communications, Inc.
Barr Films
Britannica Films
CBS/Fox Video
Cally Curtis Company
Copeland Griggs Productions
The Dartnell Corporation
Walt Disney Training & Development Programs
EFM Films
Educational Resources, Inc.
Film Communicators
Industrial Training Systems
International Training Consultants, Inc.
International Writing Institute, Inc.
McGraw-Hill Training Systems
National Educatioanal Media, Inc.
Philip Office Associates, Inc. Service
Perform, Inc.
Ramic Productions, Inc.
Roundtable Films, Inc.
Salenger, Inc.
Simon & Schuster Communications
Thaxton & Associates, Inc.
Time Life Video
The Training Files
Vantage Communications
Visucom Video Arts
Xicom, Inc.

TMDA ASSOCIATE MEMBERS

AIMS Media
Allied Film and Video
AME Inc.
ARC International Ltd.
Cine Magnetics Film & Video Laboratories
Coastline Community College (Coast Telecourses)
Consolidated Film Industries
International Tele-Film Enterprises, Ltd.
Thomas McCann & Associates of Commonwealth Films, Inc.
Media Management Services, Inc.
Modern Talking Picture Service
MPL Film and Video
National Film Board of Canada
Novo Communications
Plastic Reel Corporation of American
ROA Films
Resource Presentations
Sagotsky Multimedia
Thompson-Mitchell & Associates
Training Magazine
VCA Duplicating Corporation

SUMMARY

We are generally satisfied with the outcome of the three surveys. The information we have obtained will enable us to purchase and use materials and to advise people on our campus with more assurance than we could a year ago. Professionals in the media field cannot afford to be involved in litigation. Because certain companies will not permit us to play programs over our closed-circuit TV systems, use with continuing education classes, or display to individual carrels, we will not preview or purchase from them. A file of their catalogs and fliers will not be maintained. This should not be considered "black-balling" the companies; the intent is merely to stop purchasing materials which we cannot readily use. Programs already purchased from those companies have become a significant problem. The tapes, cassette cases, and their cards have been labeled with specific restrictions. While the possibility for error exists, these precautions and sincere efforts to follow each companies' procedures should be acceptable.

Producers have the right to specify how and with whom their materials are used. On the other hand, media professionals have an obligation to be aware of such restrictions and to negotiate the best agreements obtainable. As technology advances, producers feel the need to place restrictions which give them time to thoughtfully consider the implications for their products. We found that we can usually obtain what we need from producers, if they can legally give it to us, and if we have pursued it with courtesy, patience, and understanding.

Bibliography of Recommended Readings

Association for Educational Communications and Technology and the Association of Media Producers. *Copyright and Educational Media.* Washington, D.C.: Author, 1977.

Miller, Jerome K. *Using Copyrighted Videocassettes in Classrooms, Libraries and Training Centers.* 2nd Ed.; Friday Harbor, WA.: Copyright Information Services, 1987.

Motion Picture Association of America. Film Security Office. "Warning! 'For Home Use Only' Means Just That!" Hollywood, CA: MPA, 1981.

Richardson, A. and T. Schwartz. "What Media Managers Should Know About Copyrights." *EITV*, October, 1982.

Sinofsky, Esther R. *Off-Air Videotaping in Education: Copyright Issues, Decisions, Implications.* New York: R.R. Bowker, 1984.

Talab, Rosemary S. *Commonsense Copyright: A Guide to the New Technologies.* Jefferson, NC: McFarland, 1986.

Television Licensing Center Guides available from: TLC, 5547 N. Ravenswood Ave., Chicago, IL 60640-1199.

U.S. Copyright Office. *General Guide to the Copyright Act of 1976.* Washington, D.C.: Government Printing Office, 1977-78.

U.S. Copyright Office. *The Nuts and Bolts of Copyright.* Washington, D.C.: Government Printing Office, 1980.

Chapter 12 :

An Institutional Copyright Policy Regulating Video Use

by

Charles W. Vlcek

It is extremely important for schools to develop policies and procedures which regulate and control video use in their classrooms. The number of videocassette recorders (VCRs) in schools and homes is increasing rapidly. It has been estimated that eighty-four percent of all schools have at least one VCR in their buildings. According to a recent survey by Quality Educational Data, satellite receiving dishes have been purchased by 515 school districts in the United Stated serving 5,357 schools.[1] As budgets for instructional materials shrink and the availability of recording equipment increases, school personnel become tempted to record, duplicate and use programs from a wide variety of sources, (i.e., recorded off the air at home or school, recorded off the satellite, and from rental agencies or distributors). While the purpose of such use is laudable, the legality may be questionable. Therefore it is important that a policy exist to provide direction to

---

1   Quality Educational Data. "Educational Mailing Lists, 1987-1988," (Denver, CO: Quality Educational Data, n.d.), p. 21..

school employees and to protect the employees, administrators, and the governing body from potential litigation.

USING FILMS & VIDEO IN CLASSROOMS

Most audiovisual materials purchased or rented by educational institutions from educational instructional distributors may be displayed in classrooms without fear of copyright infringement. The copyright law provides exclusions which authorizes classroom performances of audiovisual materials under certain conditions. "Audiovisual" materials are defined in the copyright law, Public Law 94-533, Section 101, as

> [W]orks that consist of a series of related images which are intrinsically intended to be shown by the use of machines or devices such as projectors, viewers, or electronic equipment, together with accompanying sounds, if any, regardless of the nature of the material objects, such as films or tapes, in which the work is embodied.[2]

The specific exclusion which makes the use of film and video in the classroom permissible is found in Sect. 110(1) and it states:

> Notwithstanding the provisions of Section 106, the following are not infringements of copyright:
>
> (1) performance or display of a work by instructors or pupils in the course of face-to-face teaching activities of a nonprofit educational institution in a classroom or similar place devoted to instruction, unless, in the case of a motion picture or other audiovisual work, the performance, or the display of individual images, is given by means of a copy that was not lawfully made under this title, and that the person responsible for the performance knew or had reason to believe was not lawfully made;[3]

---

2   *United States Code*, Title 17, "Copyrights," Sect. 101 (Hereafter: Copyright Act.)
3   Copyright Act. Sect. 110(1).

The discussion in House Report 94-1476, page 81, clarifies that "teaching activities" exempted by Section 110(1) covers a wide variety of subjects but do not include performances or displays, whatever their cultural value or intellectual appeal, that are given for the recreational or entertainment of any part of their audience.[4]

It would appear that the above exclusion requirements of Sect. 110 and the House Report would make the display of audiovisual materials in fraternity and sorority houses, dormitories and other nonclassroom areas within an institution a violation of copyright law without appropriate clearances or licenses. To clarify these points, educational institutions need a copyright policy that give direction in these matters. The policy might begin with the following statement:

Recommended Policy Statement:

Media materials (film, video, instructional kits, etc.) purchased, rented or leased by (name) school district/institution may be used in classrooms for systematic teaching activities that relate to the established curriculum. Media materials will not be shown for recreational or entertainment purposes.

VIDEOTAPING OFF THE AIR AT SCHOOL

Off-air taping at school is permissible if several conditions have been met. First, the conditions as specified in the "Guidelines for Off-air Recording of Broadcast Programming for Educational Purposes"[5] must be followed. These guidelines (see Appendix) were developed by a negotiating committee consisting of representatives from educational organizations, copyright proprietors, and creative guilds. The guidelines provide the specific conditions that must be met when programs are to be taped from off-air sources. In addition to the guidelines other conditions must be met. First, the taping must be requested by a teacher, not a principal, librarian, or media director. A principal or librarian may not request a taping on the premise that they believe a program would be valuable for classroom use. Second, the

---

4   U.S. House of Representatives, *Report No. 94-1476*, Sect. 110(1), p. 81. (Hereafter: House Report.)
5   U.S. Congressional Record, October 14, 1981.

source from which the program is being taped must be broadcast to the "general public." That includes all programs being transmitted to homes and schools by direct station or cable transmission when a separate subscription fee is charged. This requirement makes it permissible to record programs being transmitted from most broadcasting stations and cable transmission of broadcast programs. It excludes premium or "pay television" programming available from cable systems, such as "Showtime," "Disney Channel," "Movie Channel" etc.

To retain recorded programs beyond the ten-day classroom use and forty-five day period for evaluation purposes (criteria #2 as stated in the Fair Use Guidelines), permission or a license must be obtained. Permission is sometimes available, but licensing has become a common practice. The Television Licensing Center (TLC) has been established to serve as a clearing house for obtaining licenses (see address at end of this chapter). The TLC requires schools and colleges to sign a free master license as a registration vehicle. It then provides free information to participationg institutions. Licenses are available for specific programs. The fee structure and license duration vary.

If a license is not available from TLC, permission must be obtained directly from the producer. The request should specify how long the program is to be retained, how it is to be used, who is going to use it, the source from which the material was recorded, and date it was recorded.

Recommended Policy Statement:

Programs videotaped off the air or off the cable for use in classrooms must meet the following conditions:

1. Meet the criteria specified in the "Guidelines for Off-Air Recording of Broadcast Programming for Educational Purposes" (*Congressional Record*, October 14, 1981). See appendix.

2. The taping must be at the request of a teacher.

3. The requested program source must be broadcast to the "general public" by a broadcasting station. This excludes "premium" or "pay television" channels, (i.e., "Showtime," "Disney Channel," "Movie Channel," etc.)

4. Permission or a license must be obtained and filed in the district/institution copyright office for programs that do not meet the above conditions.

VIDEOTAPING AT HOME FOR SCHOOL USE

As the number of videocassette recorders increases in homes, teachers find it convenient to record programs in the home and bring the programs to school for instructional purposes. The Sony Betamax case made it clear that non-commercial videotaping in the home is permissible as long as the recorded programs are viewed within the home and viewed by the family or a small circle of friends. While the Sony case did not address the issue of using programs taped at the classroom, there seems to be some agreement among copyright consultants that such use would be permissible if all the criteria specified in the off-air guidelines are followed. The off-air guidelines do not address the issue of where permissible taping can be made and again most authorities believe tapes could be made outside of the institution, (i.e., in the home). While there are no court cases to support that opinion, most copyright consultants believe that a strong case exists, especially if very detailed documentation of teacher request, recording date, when used, and erasure dates are required and maintained. (See illustration 1)

Recommended Policy Statement:

Video programs recorded at home by teachers may be used in the classroom if they meet all the conditions specified in "Guidelines for Off-Air Recording of Broadcast Programming for Educational Purposes" for school off-air recording and full records for each recording and use are filed in the district/institution copyright office.

VIDEOTAPING OFF THE SATELLITE

The rapid improvement in satellite antennas and their relatively low cost has made the reception of programs from satellites practical in universities, colleges, school, and homes. However, the legality of receiving and using these programs in schools is a complex issue.

The Communication Act of 1934, Title 47, *United States Code* Section 605 appears to prohibit the use of programs received by satellite unless the programs are transmitted "for use of the general public." Most programs transmitted by satellite are not targeted for the general public. They are transmitted by subscription from one location to a broadcasting station or cable operation for rebroadcast.

The Act was amended in October, 1984 to authorize the reception of satellite signals within the home if the programming is (1) not encrypted (2) a marketing system has not been established, or (3) a marketing system has been established and permission has been obtained.[6] These exemptions are limited to receptions for home use and cannot be generalized to uses outside of the home. A case might be developed paralleling home off-air taping of broadcast station or cable programs and using them in schools under the fair use criteria if the satellite home use conditions and the off-air use criteria are met and detailed records maintained. However, it would appear that until this issue is tested in the courts that permission or legal counsel be obtained before one records and uses programs from satellite without appropriate agreements.[7]

Recommended Policy Statement:

Programs may not be recorded from a television satellite unless written permission or a license agreement has been obtained and filed with the district/institution copyright office.

DUPLICATING FILMS AND VIDEO

The duplication of films or video from any source is not permissible unless written permission has been obtained or the use is specifically exempted in the U.S. Copyright law, (Title 17, *United States Code*, Section 101, et seq.). The law provides for legal copying under specific

---

6   Cable Communications Policy Act of 1984, Public Law No. 98-549, Par. 5, 98 STAT. 2779 (1984).

7   For further discussion of this topic, see Chapter IV in Vlcek, Charles W., *Copyright Policy Development: A Resource Book for Educators,* Friday Harbor, WA: Copyright Information Services. 1987.

conditions in Section 107, (Fair Use) and Section 108, (Reproductions by Libraries and Archives). It is tempting for librarians, media directors or teachers to duplicate media materials (films, videocassettes, slides, etc.) obtained legally from distributors or rental agencies for preview or classroom use. This practice is not only unethical but a violation of copyright law and is paramount to stealing, as it deprives the creators of a fair return for their investment of time and production costs. Institutions should have a clear statement within their copyright policy addressing this problem.

Recommended Policy Statement:

No media material (film, video, instructional kits, slides, etc.) purchased, leased or rented by the district may be duplicated without the producers and distributors written permission or appropriate license agreement and the document is filed in the district copyright office or the duplication is specifically exempted by the U.S. Copyright Law, Title 17, *United States Code*, Section 101, etc. seq.

CLOSED-CIRCUIT TRANSMISSIONS

Many educational institutions would like to transmit video programs to classrooms for convenience to teachers and students. As the technology improves for providing classroom remote start/stop/rewind functions from the classroom, this practice is likely to grow. A cursory review of Sect. 110(2) would appear to allow educators to transmit video programs by open or closed-circuit television transmission to classrooms.

Notwithstanding the provisions of Section 106, the following are not infringements of copyright:

. . . .

(2) performance of a nondramatic literary or musical work or display of a work, by or in the course of a transmission, if—

(a) the performance or display is a regular part of the systematic instructional activities of a governmental body or a nonprofit educational institution; and

97

(b) the performance or display is directly related and of material assistance to the teaching content of the transmission; ..[8].

However, Jerome K. Miller, a well known copyright consultant, emphasizes that a key limitation appears in the first line of Sect. 110(2): "performance of a non-dramatic literary or musical work..."

"Literary works" are works, other than audiovisual works, expressed in words, numbers, or other verbal or numerical symbols or indencia, regardless of the nature of the material objects, such as books, periodicals, manuscripts, phonorecords, films, tapes, disks, or cards, in which they are embodied.[9]

Audiovisual works are excluded from the definition of literary works, so video may not be transmitted under the Sect. 110(2) exclusion.

If one looks to the committee report issued by the House of Representatives to accompany the Copyright Revision Act of 1976 regarding the transmission of programs, the language is equally vague but one may get the impression that such transmission is permissible.

"(I)n the course of face-to-face teaching activities" is intended to exclude broadcasting or other transmission from an outside location into classrooms, whether radio or television and whether open or closed circuit. However, as long as the instructor and pupils are in the same building or general area, the exemption would extend to the use of devises for amplifying or reproducing sounds and for projecting visual images.[10]

While the first sentence of the house report statement specifically excludes broadcasting to classrooms "from an outside location," the second sentence seems to leave some room for further interpretation. Miller offers another interpretation.

---

8   Copyright Act. Sect. 110(2).
9   Copyright Act. Sect. 101.
10   House Report, p 81.

No one seems to know what the congressional committee had in mind when it wrote that section; its greatest apparent value is helping to justify the use of public address systems and remote control projectors used in large lecture halls. Whatever its purpose, this interesting piece of legislative history clearly does not supersede the law, so copyrighted videocassettes cannot be transmitted to classrooms via closed-circuit or educational broadcasts, except with the permission of the copyright proprietor.[11]

Some distributors will grant closed-circuit transmission rights free upon request but most require the purchase of a license. When it is desirable to transmit programs to classrooms, two types of licenses may be required; (1) license to transmit the program, and (2) another license to transfer film to tape if necessary. While an institution may own a print of a program on video or film format, the purchase agreement generally prohibits it from being transmitted. Therefore, a license must be purchased if it is desirable to transmit the program. A recent survey by this author of distributors of educational programs indicated that the average cost of a life of the tape transmission license is approximately $100 above the purchase price of the program.

In institutions where a large film collection exists, it may be desirable to transfer the collection to a videotape format. If so, permission or a license is required before a program can be legally transferred. Permission is often granted for out-of-print programs, if the former distributor or producer can be located. The same survey indicated that the cost for this type of license varies. The average cost is again approximately $100 but several educational distributors would sell the requester a new video copy for the same price as a license to transfer. Other distributors stated that they would negotiate the price downward based upon the number of the distributor's programs presently owned by the institution.

---

11   Miller, Jerome K., *Using Copyrighted Videocassettes in Classrooms, Libraries, and Training Centers,* 2d ed, from a manuscript copy of Chapter 3.

Recommended Policy Statement:

Media materials (film, video, instructional kits, etc.) may not be transmitted to classrooms by open- or closed-circuit television unless appropriate licenses or written permission has been obtained and filed in the district/institution copyright office. No programs will be transferred from film to tape or duplicated unless permission or a license has been obtained and filed in the district/institution copyright office.

BENEFIT PERFORMANCES

Many organizations within educational institutions hold fund raising activities. Some organizations sell admission tickets or accept donations for admission to view a video program(s) as a fund raising activity. The exemption in Sect. 110(4) appears to authorize the use of video materials for non-commercial benefit performances.

Nothwithstanding the provisions of Section 106, the following are not infringements of copyright:....

(4) performance of a nondramatic literary or musical work otherwise than in a transmission to the public, without any purpose of direct or indirect commercial advantage and without payment of any fee or other compensation for the performance to any of its performances, promoters, or organizers, if —

(a) there is no direct or indirect admission charge; or

(b) the proceeds, after deducting the reasonable costs of producing the performance, are used exclusively for educational, religious, or charitable purposes and not for private financial gain...[12]

Again, the definition of the term "literary work" appears to eliminate performances of video materials for benefit purposes as a permissible use. As previously quoted in the discussion on Closed-Circuit Transmissions, the definition of "literary works" from Sect. 101 excludes audiovisual works within its definition. Jerome K. Miller summarizes the effects of this definition as follows:

---

12   Copyright Act, Sect. 110(4).

The limitation is in the first eight words: "literary works are works, other than audiovisual works...." Because of this clause, free and benefit performances are limited to nondramatic literary or musical works — and audiovisual works are specifically excluded from this category. Some audiovisual works might be regarded as musical works, but that offers little encouragement, as phonograph records and audiotapes are identified in the copyright law as "phonorecords," and as such, receive special protection. Media purists object to identifying videocassettes as an "audiovisual works," but format fits the term as it is defined in the law.

It appears, then, the copyright act intentionally or accidentally prohibits performances of audiovisual works, including videocassettes, except under the educational exemption, the home-use exemption, the business meeting exemption, or with a license.[13]

While it appears that the definition of "literary works" prohibits performing audiovisual works for noncommercial benefits, the exclusion does form a legal basis for performing other non-audiovisual literary, nondramatic and musical works for noncommercial benefits when the conditions of Section 110(4) are satisfied.

Recommended Policy Statement:

Audiovisual works (film, video, instructional kits, etc.) may not be performed for noncommercial benefit purposes unless appropriate permission or license has been obtained and filed in the district/institution copyright office.

MAINTAINING NECESSARY RECORDS

Throughout this chapter it has been emphasized that whenever a use is not permitted by the copyright law, written permission or a license must be obtained. Failure to obtain the appropriate permission or license may place the institution's employees, management and the governing board in a potential position of litigation. All records neces-

---

13   Miller, Jerome K., Ibid.

sary to prove compliance with the copyright law must be retrievable. A convenient form for documenting compliance to the criteria is presented in Illustration 1.

To facilitate a copyright records management plan, someone within the organization should be named as the institution's copyright officer. This person should be given the responsibility and authority to develop and implement a copyright policy for the institution and maintain all copyright records. The copyright officer should do all negotiating for licenses to eliminate duplication of efforts and to assure that appropriate licenses are obtained and maintained.

Recommended Policy Statement:

An institutional copyright officer shall be appointed and given the responsibility and authority to develop, implement and manage a copyright policy, with appropriate procedures and to maintain appropriate records of permissions, agreements and licenses.

SELECTED BIBLIOGRAPHY

1. Johson, Beda, *How to Acquire Legal Copies of Video Programs,* 2d ed.; San Diego, CA: Video Resources Enterprise, 1987.

2. Miller, J. K., *Using Copyrighted Videocassettes in Classrooms, Libraries, and Training Centers,* 2d ed. Friday Harbor, WA: Copyright Information Services, 1988.

3. *Sat Guide: Cable's Satellite Magazine,* Sat. Guide, Boise, ID. 83707.

4. Sinofsky, Esther R, *Off Air Videotaping in Education: Copyright Issues, Decision, Implications,* New York: R.R. Bowker, 1984.

5. Talab, R.S., *Commonsense Copyright: A Guide to the New Technologies,* Jefferson, NC: McFarland, 1986.

6. Vlcek, Charles W., Copyright Policy Development: A Resource Book for Educators, Friday Harbor, WA: Copyright Information Services, 1987.

7. Wilkerson, Daniel J., "The Copyright Act of 1976 Served on a Satellite Dish", *Willamette Law Review,* Winter, 1985.

SELECTED ADDRESSES

1.   Television Licensing Center
5547 Ravenswood Avenue
Chicago, IL 60640
800-323-4222

2.   U.S. Copyright Office
Information and Publications Section LM-455
Library of Congress
Washington, DC 20559

3.   PBS Video
475 L'Enfant Plaza SW
Washington, DC 20024
800-424-7963

4.   ABC
Wide World of Learning, Inc.
1330 Avenue of the Americas
New York, Ny 10019
212-887-5706

5.   CBS
51 West 52nd St.
New York, NY 10019
212-975-3200

6.   CBS News
524 West 57th St.
New York, NY 10019
212-975-4321

7. NBC
    30 Rockefeller Plaza
    New York, NY 10112
    212-664-4966

Chapter 13 :

Please May We Have Written Permission?

by

Marjorie Madoff

and

Debra Mandel

This article describes problems the authors encountered in securing educational performance rights for prerecorded videocassettes sold "For Home Use Only." The problems they encountered are similar to the problems educators and librarians have encountered in securing permission to retain and use programs videotaped off the air. There is one difference though. Most distributors of home-use-only videocassettes have never been asked for educational performance rights, so they are not accustomed to handling those requests. On the other hand, many producers of television programs are accustomed to receiving requests for permission to retain programs for educational use and many of them have procedures for handling the requests. As the distributors of home-use-only videocassettes become accustomed to receiving requests for educational performance rights, they also may develop procedures for expediting requests for permission.

In the controversy over the use of "home-use-only" videocassettes, media librarians in academic libraries have attempted to track the copyright proprietors to obtain permission in writing for the educational usage specific to our needs. Although we firmly believe that academic libraries meet the requirements for educational exemption under Section 110(1), there is enough gray area in the law to make us feel vulnerable and therefore cautious so we try to obtain the double protection of written permission.[1]

We are often told how easy it is; experts advise us to simply make the phone call, or write the letter, describing our usage, and the permission will be forthcoming. In reality, numerous long distance inquiries result in little information about who actually owns the copyright. We are often shunted to "customer services" who know little and seem shocked by our questions. There are vendors, distributors, lawyers, producers, directors and authors, and no one knows who is which or where to direct the phone call.

One recent case will illustrate the confusion, although in this situation we were eventually successful, which makes it not the usual experience. As in most academic libraries, the case began when a faculty member arrived with an advertisement in hand for a videocassette which seemed perfect for her curriculum plan. She had a full-page ad describing a "How to" 30 minute tape, listed at $29.95. It was so inexpensive, that she did not understand my hesitancy, and only wanted me to complete the printed order form for her. Yet it was the low cost, that made me suspect that this was a "home-use only" videotape, although the ad did not state this. I tried, as I do so many times, to explain this "gray" area of the copyright law. I promised her that I would do my best to obtain permission for her to use this tape as an out of class assignment for her students to view in carrels in our library, which is the usage most often requested by faculty at Northeastern University. However, I explained that I would not purchase the tape without such

---

1   For an explanation of the library exemption under Sect. 110(1), see J.K. Miller, *Using Copyrighted Videocassettes in Classrooms, Libraries, and Training Centers* (2d ed.; Friday Harbor, WA: Copyright Information Services, 1987.)

permission, and that I had to have it in writing, and that it had to be for "the life of the tape". I cannot fill our collection with temporary holdings, or with any material which could leave the University vulnerable to infringement questions.

My first call was to the magazine in which the ad appeared. The receptionist seemed confused, but after two phone transfers, someone gave me the name of the distributor which I will call Home Video Company Technology, Boston, MA. No phone number was available. In the *Video Sourcebook*, I found the listing with a telephone number, and called the company, which was in California. A receptionist answered, listened to my problem, and transferred me to Customer Service. A smiling voice, whose name I quickly wrote down, said it certainly sounded to her like a reasonable use, and she did not understand why I needed any "permission". Although I agreed with her that our usage met the educational exemption, I insisted that I needed this in writing to protect ourselves from any ambiguity. She responded by asking me to write a letter. I did, and it was dated April 22. When May 20th arrived, and I had received no response of any kind, I again called the woman but I was told, as often happens, that she was no longer there. I requested customer service and a new person told me that if such a letter arrived, it would automatically be forwarded to their Legal Department, which in this case was in another city in California. She was most helpful and gave me both a phone number and a name. I called. A secretary advised me that although my letter may have been forwarded, it would be wise for me to send a second copy because "things get lost." I sent a copy of my original letter, and wrote a cover letter to the new name and the new address. Again, I waited a month with no reply. I then called the Legal Department again, and left a message for the name. No answer. A week or so later I tried again, and this time I spoke to a personable young man, who said he had my letter, and thought it was no problem to sign and return it. However, there were several obstacles: first he would need to check with the magazine to be sure they agreed, and second, The Home Video Company was possibly going to merge with a large producer, and things were generally up in the air around there, so it might take some time. He advised me to wait two weeks, and if I had still heard nothing, to call him again. I put another reminder on my calendar, and waited.

How much time and effort had been consumed so far? I, like most media librarians, do not have a secretary to write letters, make phone calls or remind me of dates. I also have to explain to my supervisor, the numerous calls from Boston to different cities in California. If I am trying to track more than one tape, all of these little events can begin to infringe on my time, my patience, and even my budget. After the two weeks, I called again, and this time, the secretary told me that she was just putting the permission letter together to send to me. About a week later, it arrived. My letter was signed, and a cover letter which sounded more legal explained that the permission was limited to the usage described.

I was quite exultant over my achievement, and ordered the tape, called the faculty member to tell her, and generally celebrated! I now have my permission letter, and my videotape, and I hope all is well, though it certainly gave me a rather anticlimactic sense of the end of my story.

When the "experts" tell me that obtaining permission is a simple matter of calling the copyright proprietor, I know better. I could describe other less successful ventures where I never located the copyright owner, or gave up in trying to reach a person, or having a letter or phone call answered. Whenever possible, I, and most of my colleagues, use the few vendors who have addressed this problem. Janus Films, distributed by The Voyager Company, clearly states that the videotapes they distribute include "public performance rights". They charge a slightly higher cost, which is legitimate and reasonable. Films, Inc. clearly identifies which of its tapes include public performance rights, and flags others which can be licensed for an additional small fee. We are delighted—the time, energy and money wasted on trying to track copyright proprietors has been a frustration for many years.

Many of my colleagues at professional meetings laugh at us for attempting to comply with a law which is so unclear that it hardly merits our attention. In the future we will support those distributors, such as the two mentioned, who are considerate enough to help us whenever possible. We also will continue to hope that the "experts" will clearly support our contention that academic libraries differ from public libraries, and that if we outline procedures to insure that these home-use-only tapes will not be used for "entertainment", we are clearly complying with both the intent and the letter of the law.

Meanwhile, we will do our best to protect our institutions by laboriously tracking down copyright proprietors and requesting written permissions. We do not expect to be successful very often.

Part IV :

Copyright Policy and Recordkeeping

Chapter 14 :

From Hanging Files to PC Files: Computerizing your Permissions Systems

by

Jeanne A. Gough

The author describes the rational and procedures for establishing computerized records for a publishing firm. The concepts can be applied to computerized permissions records for a college or school district.

With the recent Supreme Court cases of *Harper & Row* v *Nation Enterprises* and *Salinger v Random House*[1] the fear of copyright infringement has to be at the backs of the minds of all who are working on any type of publication that utilizes material from another source. Because of this increasing concern, permissions departments (or those individuals who handle permissions along with a myriad of

---

1   *Harper & Row v. Nation Enterprises* 501 F.Supp. 848, (aff'd), and *Salinger v. Random House* 81 F2nd 90 (Cert denied).

other responsibilities) are getting more work than ever. Not only are they requesting more formally, they are receiving requests and inquiries from individuals and companies who may never have considered permission a necessity.

For many, then, the process of requesting and/or granting permission to reprint has come to mean a lot of letters typed, material photocopied in triplicate or more, follow-up reminders, contracts signed and countersigned, schedules kept on bulletin boards to determine when to expect this, who is delinquent on that, etc., and increased numbers of file drawers bulging with correspondence and agreements. In short, too much paperwork taking too much time. Gone are the days (they'd better be!) of the curious phone call, the positive response, and absolutely no record of any transaction having taken place. No one can afford to be that careless in this increasingly litigious society.

The personal computer, if one was lucky or deemed important enough to receive one, enables the permissions person to at least keep lists of formulate letters which were then run off, photocopies, followed-up, etc. A little less time consuming, perhaps, but eventually just as much paperwork.

Now that word processors and p.c.'s have virtually replaced typewriters in today's offices, many more permissions people are finding it very easy to load a disk with the bits and pieces they've been filing away in folders or stuffing in drawers. Some have added software packages to their p.c.'s that enable them to be much more elaborate.

But a computerized permissions system need not be elaborate. Just being able to keep the basics on diskettes will allow for more efficiency. And even though one must continue written correspondence, the resulting information can be kept on diskette while the most important original paperwork or contracts can be stored. As one becomes more familiar and comfortable with just what granting and requesting permission is all about, then he will know just what kind of information will be necessary to include on his p.c.

Obviously, all systems will need programming; however, with this sense of what is necessary and a programmer with basic skills, your system can be set up rather easily. Very basically, you can keep letters and contracts on a system which you can fill in and print out to send to sources. You can also keep lists of fees owed to you, complimentary copies due you, and the date upon which you expect these. These could be accessed by dates so that you can be kept aware of your timetables.

The screen examples presented here are taken from a system set up on a mainframe computer. However, these examples will show you the kinds of information you can include in a permissions system. Adaptability to your own needs and available hardware and software will determine what you can do.

Screen 1

		Pub.No. 62500
62500 XYZ Publishers, Inc		Cross Ref #
Type: A	Infor Date: 07-01-88	Source: Reply
Contact name:	Marian Jones	
Title:		Permissions Manager
Department:		
Address:		123 South Main Street
City:		Anywhere
State:	MI	Zip: 12345 PH:555-555-5555
Country:		TX:
Fee Policy Date:		07-01-77

Fee Policy: Company will grant permission to reprint material for a nominal fee if used in a profit making venture. Otherwise, they won't charge us.

They Handle: RST Communications Company.

Remarks: You can begin a list of publications or other material for which you have requested permission. Add any detals pertinent to the publication or agreement.

As you can see from Screen 1, the information on and configuration of the screen can be fairly simple. Each company entry can be tagged with an identifying number (here it is 62500) which when programmed in would enable you to call up the information by number or name. The TYPE is indicated by a letter, in this case the letter "A", which signifies XYZ as a primary or parent company rather than a subsidiary. XYZ's subsidiary company, RST Communications, is TYPE X, indicating that its file will be cross referenced. This is discussed in more detail below. The date on which the information becomes known to you is then keyed in. This will serve to remind you of the timeliness of the information. The source of this information, whether it is a phone call, reply through the mail, phone book or other source also indicates the reliability of the information. Then simply follow with the pertinent name, address, etc., including telex or Fax numbers when applicable. If a fee policy has been established, that should also be indicated. This feature will enable you to figure beforehand what your permissions fees for a particular bit of material could be. If a company charges on a per-word basis, you can let an editor know just what your budget will handle. The more policies you can establish, the more accurate your guesses at costs for a book or article. A "remarks" or "notes" section is a good place to begin listing the publications, material, etc., in which this particular source controls the rights. You can also record other information pertinent to this particular source.

Screen 2

		Pub. No. 62510
62510 RST Communications Company		Cross Ref # 62500
Type: X	Info Date: 07-01-88	Source: Reply
Contact Name:	Marian Jones	
Title:	Permissions Manager	
Department:		
Address:	123 South Main Street	
City:	Anywhere	
State: MI	Zip: 12345	PH: 555-555-5555
Country:		TX:
Fee Policy Date: 07-01-88		

Fee Policy: Like parent company, will grant for a nominal fee if request is for profit-making venture. Gratis, otherwise.

As you will notice, this example (XYZ Publishers, Inc.) has a subsidiary company, RST Communications Company (see Screen 2), which is listed under "They Handle." Although these particular "dummy" companies are housed under the same roof and appear to share personnel, this is not always the case. In this day of mergers and acquisitions, it becomes very advantageous to know who handles whom. Many times companies that share "parents" do not necessarily share anything else. However, as companies pick up divisions or off prints and slide them over into their control, you will find yourself contacting one source for several publications. Having all this information at your fingertips will save returned mail, referrals, questions, etc.

The cross reference number on RST Communications Company indicates its parent company. Because the addresses and contacts for both companies are the same, you would not need to list that information twice. Keep the complete information on the parent company's file, note the cross reference number on RST's file and then access the parent company by its identifying number. This would not only save on possible typos if contacts and addresses are the same, but as changes in this information occur, you would need to update only one file.

Screen 3

Author: Smith, Mary
Date of Birth: 01-01-1952   Date of Death:
Nationality: American   Cross Reference:
Source: XYZ Publishers, Inc. Address Date: 07-01-88 Type: HO
Contact: Title:
Department:
Address: 78910 Jones Blvd.
                 Apt. 3A
                 Other Place, MI 23456
Phone: 555-555-5555   Telex:
Fee Policy:

    Remarks: Mary Smith is also employed at XYZ but prefers we contact her at her home address.

Screen 4

Source Information: XYZ Publishers, Inc. Source Date: 07-01-88
Author: Smith, Mary
Editor:

1st Title Publication: How To Program Your Computer
1st Title Year: 1987
Translator: Publisher Number: 053200
Publisher Name: Bookviews

2nd Title Publication: 2nd Title Year:
Translort: Publisher Number: 000000
Publisher Name:

U.S. Rights P.D.: N   Publisher Number: 000000
Author: Smith, Mary

        Remarks: Please contact at her home address.

Can. Rights P.D.: N   Publisher Number: 000000
Publisher Name:
Author: Smith, Mary

        Remarks: Please contact her at her home address.

Information on authors, critics, or other individuals (Screen 3) can be kept in the system much the same way as the companies. Mary Smith (access by last name) is listed with her home (HO) address. However, as the remarks indicate, she works at XYZ. Conceivably, she could have a second address screen with her office (OF) address.

The file that will inevitably be the most important and time-saving is the rights file. Once again, as Screen 4 shows, there is source information and the source date. Also listed are the publication, publisher, year of publication, and the controlling party of the reprint rights. In this case, it is the author. More often than not, it would be the publisher, whose identifying number would be indicated. A"Y" after either U.S. RIGHTS P.D.: or CANADIAN RIGHTS P.D.: would mean that the book, publication, or other material is in the public domain and rights need not be secured. Sometimes this fact is obvious by the publication date. However, occasionally a rights holder fails to renew the copyright in his title (pre-1978 publication date) and it subsequently falls into the public domain. This is information that involves initial research but then is readily accessible. these files can be accessed by author name or title of material. This information can also be kept, in shortened form, on the publisher's or individual's record.

All this information can be adjusted, of course, to keep track of those companies and individuals who contact you for permission. The rights file can hold all the publications or material for which you have rights, or which you publish but are controlled by the author. The notes on the publisher or individual files can list your publication for which they have requested permission to reprint, the fee you charged, etc.

Again, the system need not be elaborate, although it should be easily adaptable. In this day and age, when copyright laws come up for scrutiny on a regular basis, intellectual property becomes part of trade and tariff talks, and copyright policy makers constantly add to their list of questionable registrations, permissions personnel must remain as up to date, accurate, and adaptable as their systems.

Having answers at your fingertips saves time, space, money, and inevitably, aggravation. As stated earlier, you will still need to maintain written correspondence with your sources. However, storing a letter or two and a contract while transferring all other information onto a p.c. will undoubtedly enable you to do away with a few file cabinets, get rid of whatever typewriters are still floating around, and, generally astound everyone with your efficiency.

Chapter 15 :

An Annotated Bibliography

by

Ruth R. Rains

*When duplication and performance rights for television programs
are not available from the Television Licensing Center, the rights must be
obtained from the copyright owner. The owner is usually the firm that
produced the program. The producers' addresses frequently do not appear in the credits, so they must be located through other sources. The following directories are useful for locating television producers.*

Educational Film/Video Locator. 3rd ed. New York: Consortium of University Film Centers and R.R. Bowker, 1986, 3115 pages,
two vols.

Identifies approximately 150,000 film and video programs, with
subject index and an indicator of which consortium members own
prints. Producer/Distributor index runs about 24 pages. Does not include phone numbers of producers or distributors, but phone numbers
of libraries owning prints are given. This book gives producer information not available elsewhere. Price approximately $150.00. Fourth edi-
tion due 1988.

Film and Video Finder (NICEM). 1st ed.; Albuquerque: National Information Center for Educational Media, A Division of Access Innovations, Inc., 1987, about 2900 pages, in three vols.

Represents about 90,000 titles, indexed by subject and title. Includes a Producer/Distributor index with some addresses, no phone numbers, running 71 pages. Also available on-line through DIALOG, as well as on CD-ROM. Printed editions sells for about $300.

Film/Video Canadiana, 1985-1986. Montreal: National Film Board of Canada, 1986.

Published every two years, containing the Canadian productions of those years. Current edition contains approximately 3,000 titles. Equipped with six indices: subject, director, producer, production company, features, co-productions. Includes a directory of Canadian producers with addresses and phone numbers. $40., payable to the Receiver General of Canada.

Variety's Complete Home Video Directory. New York: R.R. Bowker Company, 1988, 852 p.

Approximately 25,000 titles, indexed by title, genre, closed-caption, cast/director, awards, producer/distributor, services/suppliers. Indexes tabbed for convenience. Producer/distributor index runs 27 pages, includes addresses and phone numbers. Focus is feature films. About $105.

Video Sourcebook. 9th Ed. New York: National Video Clearinghouse, 1987, 2359 pages, in one vol.

Approximately 53,000 programs with about 1,000 sources. Subject index, cast index, program source index. Program source index runs 26 pages, includes addresses, phone numbers, and formats available. Published annually. Tends to be among the most current. About $200.

Videolog. San Diego: Trade Service Publications, Inc.

Loose-leaf, updated regularly throughout the year. Includes formats, standards, MPAA ratings, award indicators. Sections as follows: New Releases, Directory of Titles, Directory of Stars, Directory of Directors, Adventures, Children's, Comedies, Dramas, Musical and Performing Arts, Religious, Science Fiction/Horror, Westerns, Foreign Films, Sports/Recreation, Education/General Interest, Adult Audience, Closed Captioned. Cost $150/yr. It is sold only to video retailers; it can be examined in many video stores.

About The Authors

Brenda Coto was previously the Director of the Television Licensing Center in Chicago. She is now associated with AIMS Media in Evanston, IL.

Dr. John A. Davis is the Director of Media Services at Washington State University in Pullman, WA.

Dr. Marvin Davis is the Director of Media Services at Area Education Agency 11 in Johnston, IA.

Jeanne Gough is a Permissions & Production Manager at Gale Research Inc. in Detroit, MI, as well as Chairpersom of the New York Rights & Permissions Group.

Mary Jo James is the Director of University Media Services at Middle Tennessee State University in Murfreesboro, TN and the Executive Director of the Tennessee State Board of Regents, Media Consortium.

Marjorie Madoff is Director of the Learning Resources Center at Northeastern University, Boston, MA.

Debra Mandel is Director of Media Services at Wentworth Institute of Technology in Boston, MA.

Dr. Jerome K. Miller is the President of Copyright Information Services in Friday Harbor, WA.

Dr. LaVerne W. Miller is the Director of the Office of Special Instructional Services at Montgomery College in Takoma Park, MD.

Paula Morrow is a freelance writer who specializes in church and video issues who lives in Springfield, MO.

Dr. Ruth R. Rains, is a bibliographic specialist at the University of Illinois Film and Video Center in Champaign, IL.

Dr. Charles W. Vlcek is the Director of Media Services at Central Washington University in Ellensburg, WA.

Dr. M. Patricia Webb is the Coordinator of Instructional Media at the Northeast Campus of Tarrant County Junior College in Hurst, TX.

Index

NOW AVAILABLE FROM COPYRIGHT INFORMATION SERVICES:

> **Leonard D. DuBoff is a well-known attorney who specializes in copyright and business law. He has established a splendid reputation for his ability to explain the law IN PLAIN ENGLISH.**

Leonard D. DuBoff, *The Law (In Plain English) for Craftspeople* $9.95

Covers trademarks, contracts, consignments, working at home, taxes, copyright, insurance, product liability, collections, forms of organization, and how to find a lawyer.

"I can't imagine that anyone in the crafts business would want to pass this book up." *PopularWoodworker*

"[It] should be read by every craft professional and small business owner. It could make the difference between success and failure." *Fiberarts*

Leonard D. DuBoff, *Business Forms and Contracts (In Plain English) for Craftspeople* $14.95

Ready-to-copy forms for copyrights, licenses, consignments, commissions, taxes, craft-show sales, mail- order sales, warranties, disclaimers, leases, incorporation, etc.

"The author has a unique knack for providing sound information about the law without resorting to legal mumbo jumbo." Carol Sederstrom

"This is a book which I plan to buy for my own library, and I would recommend it to teachers, craftsmen, and artists for its clear explanations of a very complex side of our work. It may become the most valuable book you own." Lillian V. Geer, in *Needle Arts*

Leonard D. Duboff, *The Law (In Plain English) for Small Businesses* $9.95

Covers business organization, contracts, the business plan, taxes, consignments, collections, insurance, franchising, multi-level marketing, consumer protection laws, trademarks, estate planning, and going public.

> "The book is clearly written, and it sould be kept close at hand for anyone imnvolved in a small business."
> William H. Becker

> "[L]ibrary patrons interested in acquiring an overview of the legal aspects of the business world will certainly appreciate the wealth of data offered here."   *Booklist*

Leonard D. Duboff, *The Law (In Plain English) for Writers* $9.95

Covers contracts, agents, copyright, libel, invasion of privacy, taxes, self-publishing, using a lawyer, and organizing as a business.

> "Almost any question you may have about the law and writing is discussed in clear and simple language"
> Jean M. Auel

> "DuBoff has produced a readable guide, without being simplistic, on a subject many writers want to put aside. His style is lively, and the book, surely needed."
> *Academic Library Book Review*

ORDER ALL FOUR

DuBOFF TITLES AND

RECEIVE A 10%

DISCOUNT

A COPYRIGHT PRIMER FOR EDUCATIONAL AND INDUSTRIAL MEDIA PRODUCERS

by Dr. Esther R. Sinofsky

"This book was written in response to requests by media specialists who wanted a reliable information about copyright issues in producing film, video, and multi-image programs. After receiving many requests for a book of this nature, I prepared detailed specifications for the book and asked Dr. Sinofsky to write it. She spent almost two years working on the book. The result is a splendid book that will answer media producers' questions about the copyright law. I gladly recommend this book to every media producer."   Jerome K. Miller

Includes: A Producer's Copyright Checklist and "Sinofsky's Rules of Thumb"

1988   ISBN: 914143-12-3   LC: 87-15423   236 P   CIP   C loth $29.95

USING COPYRIGHTED VIDEOCASSETTES IN CLASSROOMS, LIBRARIES, AND TRAINING CENTERS

by Dr. Jerome K. Miller

Challenges statements that videocassettes labeled for "Home Use Only" may not be used in classrooms and school media centers.

States that "Home Use Only" labels on videocassettes are not legally binding.

States that unlicensed video showings in church meeting rooms are illegal.

Describes the "business-meeting exemption" for showing videocassettes.

Discusses the Glickman copyright bill authorizing video showings in hospitals.

Provides a checklist for videocassette performance license.

Describes "cease-and-desist letters" to stop video showings.

1988 ISBN: 914143-14-X   LC: 87-24572 128 P   CIP   Cloth $19.95

NEW COPYRIGHT WORKSHOPS ON AUDIO CASSETTES:

An audiocassette tape and a full set of handounts will be available in February for Dr. Jerome K. Miller's 1989 video and computer copyright workshops:

VIDEO/COPYRIGHT SEMINAR, 1989
COMPUTER/COPYRIGHT SEMINAR, 1989

Each seminar is shipped in a library album and contains:
- one C-60 audio cassette tape,
- one booklet of official documents, and
- "Straight Facts," Dr. Millers executive summary

$24.89 each   Available: February, 1989

Order   Both   Seminars   And   Receive   A   Ten   Percent   Discount

NOW IN ITS SECOND PRINTING:

COPYRIGHT POLICY DEVELOPMENT: A RESOURCE BOOK FOR EDUCATORS

by Dr. Charles W. Vlcek

Includes step-by-step instructions for preparing an institutional copyright policy. Checklists and six sample policies are included, plus a chapter on videotaping off the satellite.

1987   ISBN: 914143-06-5   CIP   Clothbound   165 pages $19.45

CHURCH COPYRIGHT SEMINAR

by Dr. Jerome K. Miller

Explains changes in the copyright law that apply to churches and church schools. Treats video and music issues.

One audio cassette and several booklets in a vinyl album. 1987 $24.87